Affirmation Toolbox

Over 150 Different, Powerful, Action-packed Affirmation Tools to Help Y-O-U Manifest Your Desires!

Dr. Anne Marie Evers
www.affirmationtoolbox.com

Published in Canada by Affirmations International Publishing Company in 2012
All rights reserved including the right to reproduce this book or any portion thereof in any form.

ISBN# 1926995082
ISBN# 978-1-926995-08-3

Queries Regarding Rights and Permissions

Dr. Anne Marie Evers
Affirmations International Publishing Company
4559 Underwood Avenue
North Vancouver, BC
Canada   V7K 2S3

Toll-Free: 1-877-923-3476
Fax: 1 -604-904-1127

Email: anne@annemarieevers.com
               annemarieevers@shaw.ca

Websites: www.annemarieevers.com
               www.affirmationtoolbox.com
               www.annemarieschapel.com
               www.cardsoflife.com

TABLE OF CONTENTS

YOUR AFFIRMATION TOOLBOX

Note: This book may be set up differently from other books you have and are reading. You will notice that some of these Affirmation Tools are repeated, and the Affirmation Tools are recorded individually in the Table of Contents so you can access the help you need almost instantly. This is done for quicker and easier reference to the *particular* Affirmation Tool that you need in various situations.

i

TABLE OF CONTENTS

ABOUT THE AUTHOR

Dr. Anne Marie Evers is an Ordained Minister, Doctor of Divinity, Best-Selling Author; CEO of Affirmations International Publishing Company, Senior Talk Show Host on www.contacttalkradio.com--The *Dr. Anne Marie Evers Show*, Columnist, International Motivational Speaker, Affirmation Coach, Cards of Life Reader and more.

How I became known as the 'Affirmations Doctor'

One evening several years ago when I was a guest on Nicole Whitney's radio show, she left the recording studio and came back quickly about four seconds before she was to be on air, slid into her chair and said, "Now we are back with the Affirmations Doctor!" We were both a little surprised and then listeners started calling in asking to speak to the 'Affirmations Doctor,' so I became affectionately known as the *Affirmations Doctor*. Little did I know then that years later I would actually become a Doctor of Divinity! Since that time, having spent years completing my Ministerial studies, I received my Doctorate of Divinity in July 24th 2005.

Some Comments from the Media

...In *Nicole Whitney's* own words, "Dr. Anne Marie Evers has been a regular at 'News for the Soul' shows and events for many years. She is truly a Master in her field. She has inspired positive change in the lives of thousands. I believe that everyone following the Affirmation methods in her books and workshops is going to see results in his or her life. I like to call it '*Real Life Magic*.' If you are actually doing them, Affirmations HAVE to work!"

Nicole Whitney is founder and co-host of 'News for the Soul,' an online positive news broadcast center, global community, and consciousness movement for like minds and a live life-changing talk radio show airing in Vancouver and around the world. Nicole has officially named Anne Marie Evers as 'The Affirmations Doctor.'

. . . . "Dr. Anne Marie Evers' books and *Cards of Life* have always and will always be a part of our life as they are very powerful tools to create the life we want. When she comes on the radio, the listeners' feedback is awesome and they always ask for her return. We lovingly call her 'The Affirmations Doctor' because she prescribes Affirmations like a doctor prescribes rest and relaxation. Blessings to you." **Cameron and Lucia Steele,** Contact Talk Radio Hosts Seattle, WA.

Note: *All through this book and all my books, I always repeat my very own Affirmation at the end of each chapter –* **Affirmations When Properly Done Always Work!** *And they* **DO** *– sometimes not in our time frame or as we think they should, but they always work!*

Message from the Author

Imagine Over 150 Different Affirmation Tools at Your Disposal!

Note: Due to popular demand and numerous requests from you, my readers, clients and others, I have put these Affirmation Tools together in one book. Use this as your reference book to refer to whenever you wish.

I have created over 150 different Affirmation Tools for you in this book. I have personally done each and every Affirmation Tool and many of my family, friends, readers, etc. have also used many of them with great success.

I use these Affirmation Tools on a daily basis. They are my constant friends and helpers and I could not imagine my life without them. You will notice that I have repeated a few of the Affirmation Tools to be used in various sections as applicable to make it easier for you to access that particular Affirmation Tool quickly.

When you are experiencing a challenge in your life, don't struggle, worry and fret about what to do—just go to your Affirmation Toolbox book, select the appropriate tool, use it and reap the benefits.

These very simple, yet powerful, tools can be used instantly. No searching, ordering and waiting for a book or product to arrive! It is my Nightly Affirmation/Prayer that these simple, yet powerful, Affirmation Tools work for you successfully as they have for my family, friends, associates, readers and me.

Many people, like me, need simple, effective, quick, easy-to-use tools to handle uncertain situations. Some of these Affirmation Tools are so simple you may have overlooked them on your life journey. You could be already using many of them, just not recognizing them as Affirmation Tools.

Many of them have been mentioned in my other books, but I wanted to create a quick reference of the Affirmation Tools for you.

These wonderful one-of-a-kind Affirmation Tools are NOT to be used in place of your doctor's advice and/or prescription, but are only to be used as additional support.

I wish to dedicate this book to my dear friend and colleague, Hilary Lee, who worked long hours organizing and creating the setup of this book. Thank you, thank you, thank you, Hilary. I also dedicate this book to every person anywhere who is on a similar path, or those who are new to this way of life and eager to learn.

It is my hope and Affirmation/Prayer for you, dear reader, that this book will provide some important Affirmation Tools that you can and will use to create what you wish for in your life; for example—radiant health; perfect, lasting successful career; that perfect, loving life partner; abundance of money; more friends; material things; and, most of all, greater personal and spiritual growth, which is what life is *really* all about. When doing Affirmations and using the Affirmation Tools, exercises, and methods in this book, always be conscious of the real reason we are here, on planet earth, at this particular time. I believe the real reason is to learn, evolve, grow and become the very best we can be! And then to help others that *wish* to do the same. Let us always strive to be the very best we can be and always be conscious of others' opinions and ways. In other words — Live and Let Live.

As you read these words, please keep an open mind and allow these words, the ones that resonate with you and accept, to sink deep into your subconscious mind where they will be stored for all time.

Sometimes when we learn some exciting, interesting information we are quick to offer to share it with our friends and it could be that they are not on the same thinking level. Please be aware that every person grows at his or her own speed. At times, you may try to read a book and cannot get into it, so you put it on the shelf and pick it up later, sometimes years later, and find it is exactly what you need to know at that time. Have the words in the book changed since you first tried to get into reading it? No, of course not! You and only you are the one that has changed, grown, and evolved.

DISCLAIMER

This information is provided to give you ideas on different Affirmation Tools and how to use them to help you on your life journey. This information is based on my life experiences and from many of my readers who have used these Affirmation Tools with great success.

Of course, the results differ with each individual, depending on how much time is put into doing them and each person's individual belief system.

You may wish to check with your medical practitioner, etc. before doing these Affirmations, exercises, methods and/or using these Affirmation Tools. The reason I point this out is that several of my readers tell me that they feel so good when they do Affirmations on a regular basis that they are thinking of cutting down on their medications or stopping them altogether. I always **stress** to follow your doctor's orders and keep on taking your medication UNTIL your doctor advises you otherwise. Use these powerful Affirmation Tools, exercises, methods, etc. as additives. Always take this information and add it to your own 'common sense and sense of balance.'

About the phrase 'Affirmations When Properly Done Always Work!' —

You will notice that it is my own Affirmation that appears after every section–and after each chapter in my books and writings.

Affirmations When Properly Done Always Work!
(Sometimes not in our time frame or
as we think they should!)

CARDS OF LIFE

The images in this book are taken from *The Cards of Life*. The Cards of Life were created by Dr. Anne Marie Evers.

The set consists of seventy-two Cards with twelve sections and five cards and one Major Card in each section, making a total of seventy-two Cards.

When used properly, *The Cards of Life* can and do suggest future events and offer wisdom from your *Higher Self*. They also give guidance and assist in handling life's challenges and taking the guesswork out of problem solving. These Cards are used very successfully doing readings for self and with individuals, groups, parties & for recreational purposes.

Please visit www.cardsoflife.com to learn more about these wonderful Cards. As well you can purchase *The Cards of Life Certification Course* and learn how to start your own home business.

Happy Affirming

INTRODUCTION

Affirmations: Your Passport to Happiness

Congratulations on getting this book into your hands. It is your passport to attracting what you want in your life. As I stated previously, the methods and tools incuded in this book have been used with great success by my readers and friends for many years. I have personally done each and every exercise presented here. Some of these tools and exercises have not been included in my previous books or other writings.

People have been asking for a quicker way to attract what they want into their lives, and that is what this is all about.

Are you at the point in your life where you are wondering why you are here, what your purpose is, and what more there could be to life? If so, this book is written for you! These tools and simple, effective exercises will enable you to take control of your life and make positive changes.

All of these suggestions, tools, methods, exercises, and Affirmations are working with your subconscious mind and with the natural and wondrous power which is within you and every person, and which is just waiting to be acknowledged and used.

I find it important that, in the beginning, when you start doing your Affirmations, methods, etc. for your own personal growth and attainment, it is best to keep it a secret. After your Affirmations have manifested as affirmed, then it is time to share with others. You see, at times, when we share what we are doing with another person or persons they may say, "Oh, that won't work; I tried it; A few words certainly will not make a difference; Oh, are you off again on another tangent?" and other statements, and the result could be that you believe them, become discouraged and do not do the work required to make your Affirmations manifest as affirmed for you. Remember, this is YOUR LIFE—*you* are the engineer, creator, and only decision-maker in your Universe!

You are here to learn, evolve, and grow. You are a co-creator with God, with absolute control over your thoughts and, therefore, over your life. No one can think your thoughts for you, nor can you think thoughts for another person. Using the tremendous power of your mind, you can become a magnificent creator and a magnet for all that you desire.

Life Is a Smorgasbord

When you go to a buffet dinner or smorgasbord, you are not waited on. *You have to get up and get your food yourself.*

You have to decide what you want to eat, and then take the appropriate action of putting that food on your plate and taking it to your table. This is similar to making decisions in your life and choosing what Master Affirmations to create to bring positive changes in your life: that certain person, optimum health, more friends, abundant wealth, perfect career, forgiveness, love and harmony in your life.

Don't be like some people who just sit there and wait, saying, "God/Creator will give it to me when He decides to." I believe God gave us each a brain and mind to think, and the gift of free will. It is high time we start taking responsibility for our thoughts, words, and actions.

Important Note

Please read and study this book with excitement, enthusiasm, and with an open mind. (Even a parachute is useless in the air unless it opens.) I have heard it said that the most expensive thing in the world is a closed mind.

This information was taken from what I have read, studied, learned, and heard over the years, and from the feedback of numerous readers worldwide via telephone calls, emails, fax, and snail mail. Some of the methods included here may seem a little 'far out.' to you, but remember the old saying, "Don't knock it until you have tried it!"

This book is divided into 2 main sections:

Part 1 looks at the Affirmation process itself, providing you with the fundamental information you need to understand how Affirmations work. It also shows you how to apply it to your own life so you can immediately get started on creating your own successes.

Part 2 is an alphabetical compilation of the Affirmation Tools and exercises I use and recommend to make Affirmations even more powerful, successful, and fun!

Affirmations – Your Passport to Happiness

So what are Affirmations in a nutshell? Simply put, they are a means by which you and God/Universal Mind/ Creator/Higher Self, or whomever you believe in, collaborate together. (There are a few different ways to do this.) Here, in this book, the focus is on how to create powerful and practical Affirmations. You can learn to turn 'potential and your intention' into reality!

Because it will be a partnership between you and God/ Universal Mind/Creator/Higher Self, or whomever you believe in, you will never need to worry about the modus operandi (the way it happens). You know the **WHAT** that you want, and God/Universal Mind/ Creator/Higher Self know the **HOW**.

Do you need to worry about **HOW** to manifest whatever it is that you want? No. The Affirmation process itself does the — figuring out how. Your responsibility is to affirm, believe, take the first action, be patient and then to wait for the answer to come to you, and finally, *to take the appropriate action on it when it does.*

Note: Wherever AMCAM is used, it is referring to *Anne Marie's Contract Affirmation Method.*

Basic Questions Answered!

What?

Affirmations are similar to prayers, wishes, or goals. They are decrees, commands, statements, etc. stating exactly what you desire.

Where?

You can do AMCAM absolutely anywhere, in your home, office, car while waiting for a light to change, in your doctor's office, or while waiting in line at the bank. It is endless.

When?

You can do Affirmations anytime you choose, but I feel the most powerful times to do them are first thing in the morning and last thing before you go to sleep. When you read them over just before going to sleep it allows the words to sink deep into your subconscious mind.

Why?

We do Affirmations to change our lives to be as we wish them to be to realize our dreams: to attract that special life partner; have an abundance of monies, radiant health, an exciting career; facilitate forgiveness; improve relationships with family members and friends; develop more self-esteem; experience spiritual growth, and much, much more.

Who?

Anyone can do Affirmations, from small children to senior citizens. I have a five-year-old girl doing Affirmations and a great, great grandmother of 103!

How?

By learning and using the 5 Building Blocks, and doing the 5-step Affirmation Process in which you will learn all about these in Part One of this book.

When you do the Affirmation Process properly, you will discover how to do the following:

- » Recognize, verbalize, and write out your goals (Affirmations)
- » Improve your relationships with self and others
- » Attract the perfect, lasting successful career
- » Attract that special person (mate)
- » Handle and overcome fear and negative habits
- » Attract health, wealth, and happiness
- » Use thoughts to create miracles
- » Use the wondrous power of your subconscious mind
- » Forgive everyone and everything that has ever hurt you
- » Forgive, love, respect, and approve of yourself
- » Believe in yourself
- » Meditate and become peaceful
- » Reduce your weight and maintain your ideal figure
- » Develop self-esteem
- » Have peace of mind

- » Become more spiritual
- » Enjoy optimum health
- » Be more patient
- » Change your life as you decree
- » Face and accept death — the final destination and much, much more

Affirmations When Properly Done Always Work!

Part 1

CHAPTER 1
HOW AFFIRMATIONS WORK!

Throughout the next several chapters I'd like to tell you about:

» The building blocks on which the success of your Affirmations rests
» The steps of the Affirmation Process itself
» The important rules to follow when doing Affirmations

In this chapter, let's start by looking at some of the building blocks – they are the cornerstones of the Affirmation process and *the reason why Affirmations work*

Creative Visualization and the Power of the Mind (Seeing Mind Pictures)

Have you ever come across someone who said they liked to use visualization to succeed? Were you wondering what they were talking about? They were turning 'potential' into reality! The reality they pictured became the reality they lived.

What is the greatest power that has ever been discovered? Nuclear energy? The power of wealth or fame? I believe it is the power of your thoughts and mind. Thought is creative and it is the first and most crucial stage in the development of any new idea, invention, business, or other venture that becomes reality.

Thoughts are living things. When thoughts are held in the mind, they form a life of their own and attract other similar thoughts. We cannot afford the luxury of one negative thought. Thoughts are things. Thoughts are very powerful. Even your smallest, most insignificant thoughts are important and they are influencing everyone and everything around you.

Through thought, your mind can be programmed at will—and reprogrammed as frequently as required. As the most powerful and transformative tools at our disposal, thoughts must be used wisely if we are to create what we want out of life—the life we really desire.

Like always attracts like. Think about success and you attract successful people. You are a great thought-magnet, whether you like it or not. Mental currents are just as real as circuits of magnetism and circuits of electricity. Each kind of thought has its own rate, degree, and character of motion. You attract your own kind of thought wave to you and you repel your opposite.

Thought transference is the phenomenon whereby one person tunes into and grasps another's thoughts without any evident, visible means of communication. This process is also known as mind-reading or mental telepathy. Your thoughts and desires are actively transmitted to those around you at the subconscious level—beyond your conscious awareness. The resulting force of suggestion is very powerful. We all have this power of suggestion over others through the thought waves and patterns we are continually broadcasting.

Our thoughts affect others and the world around us. Similar to electricity, thought transference requires a sender and a receiver. You may wonder why you receive a particular thought from the thousands of other thoughts being transmitted at that very moment. In most cases, you receive *only* those thought vibrations to which you are emotionally attuned at that moment. If you are unhappy or depressed, for example, you will attract this type of thought.

Thought into Form

Your concentrated thought—when accompanied by a matching clear, colorful mental picture, filled with feeling and belief—always makes an impression upon the subconscious mind and it, in turn, sends that impression to the Universal Mind, which always responds.

The Creative Universal Mind cannot refuse to take the form your thoughts give it. It does not differentiate between so-called good and bad thoughts, and it knows only to multiply and return to you that which you have affirmed by your thinking, actions, and Affirmations.

If you pour water into a Jell-O mold and then add jelly powder, when the Jell-O is set it takes on the shape of the container. This is the way with our thoughts; they take on the shape of our feelings and emotions. So be sure to keep your thoughts positive, uplifting and happy.

You are always giving life, knowingly or unknowingly, to conditions and situations in your life, whether they are negative or positive. This energy takes the form that we give it. We are all immersed in a thought atmosphere that is a direct result of what we have thought, affirmed, or done.

Although thoughts cannot be seen by the human eye, the vibrations they emit can be registered by an MRI (Magnetic Resonance Imaging) machine. This device identifies the area of the brain that is being fired when the thought is experienced, allowing doctors to see thoughts as they occur and change in the physical brain. Such technology is enhancing our understanding of how thoughts affect our lives.

The processes of the human mind constitute one of the greatest unsolved mysteries of the Universe, yet most of us take our minds very much for granted. We think, act, and live, rarely stopping to think about how the mind works or how we control it. Affirmations (whereby we repeatedly state our desires so that they become imprinted upon the subconscious mind) represent the key to unlocking the secret door to mind-power.

In this book, you will be learning how to use this unlimited, inexhaustible power to create your heart's desires. To do this requires consciousness—a state of mindful awareness, alertness, and aliveness in the present moment. You become what you are in life from what you are in consciousness. To be conscious is to think, and with a positive focus, you attract good things and happy experiences to you. When you lower your consciousness, you give away your power and attract thoughts, situations, events, and people that reinforce this lack of power. The world within creates the world without. Everything you find in your world *without* was first created in your world *within*.

Two Minds

You have **one** mind with two distinct yet interrelated functional characteristics.

> » One is the conscious, objective, outward, or waking state
> » The other is subconscious, subjective, and inward

To understand how Affirmations work through the use of your conscious and subconscious mind, it is necessary to discuss some of the mind's functions and powers.

The Conscious Mind

The conscious mind is your objective mind and deals largely with the external world. This part of the mind has the power to reason and to decide what is right or wrong. It is the source of all thoughts, concepts, and ideas. The conscious mind's chief powers are reason, judgment, logic, form, calculation, and moral sense. The conscious mind also sets in motion the creative power of the subconscious mind. I refer to it as the 'Captain of a ship' who gives the orders.

The conscious mind is the *one and only force* to which the subconscious mind responds. It tells the subconscious mind what is required — which is one of its most important functions. The subconscious mind controls the conditions and experiences of your life. Through your conscious mind, you can clearly and specifically tell your subconscious mind what is desired.

The Subconscious Mind

(I like to call it the Magic Genie.)

Your subconscious mind is like a highly sophisticated computer. When you were born, it began to record every feeling, action, thought, or word in your world. You accepted some information from your parents, teachers, peers, and others — all of whom had their own weaknesses and negative patterns. I refer to the subconscious mind as the 'crew' who obey the 'Captain's' orders immediately and without question.

7

The subconscious mind can also be compared to a bank where you make daily *thought deposits*. These thought deposits grow and become your memory, which represents the basic raw material for new thoughts and ideas.

Your subconscious mind knows more about you than anyone. It can change its viewpoints, often retaining or reverting back to childhood ideas, concepts, and beliefs. It stores your own interpretation of reality. If something very important happened to you at age 14, for example, your subconscious mind may continue to see that event from a 14-year-old perspective.

Your subconscious mind represents the sleeping or subjective state. It is dependent on the information received from the conscious mind and is not normally in direct contact with the outside world. One of its roles is to handle all involuntary functions of the body, such as heartbeat, breathing, circulation, blood flow, and digestion without any instruction from anyone. This mind is beyond space and time, with many powers, including inspiration, imagination, organization, intuition, emotion, certitude, deduction, suggestion, and memory. It is a part of the Universal Mind, which is also timeless, ageless, and boundless.

The Universal Mind is all-powerful and all-knowing. The Universal Mind is the totality of all minds in existence, including God's mind. It is everywhere and within you and its nature is spiritual. Think how honored we are to have the capability of God's mind within us. Realizing I am a co-creator with God makes me feel humble and full of gratitude and opens a whole new dimension of creative possibility.

Isn't it exciting to know the subconscious mind contains every element necessary to manifest every one of your desires, goals, or Affirmations? You can turn on the switch in your mind, redirecting your mental processes to change from a negative mode to a positive one. There is no object, goal, or Affirmation too small or too big for the Universal Mind to manifest. The Universal Mind will give you anything you desire, but it does not deliver it to you in a package or by courier.

It acts on people, situations, and circumstances. You need patience, faith, and perseverance while waiting for your wishes to be granted, and you will need to be open to receiving whatever gifts are given to you. You know *what* you desire and the Universal Mind knows *how* to bring it to you. Nothing is impossible. You can control the thoughts you think and transmit them to your subconscious mind which, in turn, is part of the Universal Mind.

Thinking in Pictures

Thinking in pictures is one of the basic activities of the human mind. Centuries ago, cave dwellers used creative visualization. They painted pictures of the animals they wished to hunt on the cave walls. They even practiced throwing actual spears at the drawings; some of those marks can still be seen on the cave walls. Creative imagery (visualization) is the first language of the subconscious mind. Affirmations (words) are the second language. It is important to speak to your subconscious mind in a language it understands and to which it can respond. This language is imagination and creative visualization.

Creative visualization involves using your imagination to create the manifestation of your desire; it is a natural power we all possess, whether we are aware of it or not. It is a subjective experience that uses imagery and imagination. The image can be a real event or a totally imaginary one. Both create the same changes in the body.

The images your mind receives from your mental world are just as real as an event actually taking place. When you practice creative visualization and imaging, you are actually transporting yourself into the future. You put yourself into a situation that has not yet taken place. Since your mind does not know the difference between a real event and an imagined event, it accepts your visualization as truth.

All things come to people according to the pictures they form and hold in their minds. The practice of creative visualization is extremely powerful. To change your world, change the way you picture it and the results will follow. Replace negative mental images with positive ones. When images in the mind are combined with Affirmations, the combination greatly enhances the mind's ability to manifest the object of your desire. God/Universal Mind/Creator/Higher Self looks and takes notice when you tap directly into the power of the subconscious mind. God/Universal Mind/Creator/Higher Self understands it, your subconscious understands it, the Universe understands it, and so the thing you want is created. Creative visualization changes the images that you've held that created the *lack* of what you wanted in the first place. And Affirmations create a very specific definition of what is best to put in their place.

The Law of Attraction

The Law of Attraction is the name that is often given to this universal truth — *that you have the power to draw to you whatever you focus and concentrate on.* In fact, the Law of

Attraction is always turned on — *you cannot turn it off.* The thoughts, feelings, and attitudes held in your mind form a life of their own, sending out a frequency of vibration that attracts more of the same. This gives you the power to create your future.

What is happening in your life *now* actually originated from the ideas, thoughts, and beliefs you have been holding from your life experiences. What you are thinking today is creating your tomorrow. *Through the Law of Attraction each thought seeks its own kind.*

You attract what you concentrate on, just as surely as a magnet attracts metal. It is, therefore, important to fill your mind with constructive, positive thoughts. When you associate with negative people, it is possible to graft your mind to their lower-thought atmosphere and thought patterns. The mind absorbs the thoughts with which it is most associated. You can, however, choose what to think, listen to, talk about, and read. You can choose to live in love and light, rather than in fear and darkness. When you become committed to thinking positively, fear and negativity cease to be your jailer.

Fill yourself with positive thoughts and watch miracles occur in your life on a daily basis. When problems (I prefer to call them opportunities) occur in your life, ask yourself, "What must I be thinking to create this chaos?" The ability to think is the key to accessing the Universal Mind and realizing your goals.

Affirmations When Properly Done Always Work!

CHAPTER 2
AFFIRMATIONS-THE SPECIFICS

What Are Affirmations?

Affirmations are similar to prayers, wishes, or goals—only they are more structured, focused, and specific.

They are also orders for change, a decree, or statement. *This is your order to the Universe.* Simply put, the basis of all Affirmations is positive thinking, belief, and faith. To affirm is to *make firm*.

If you have ever blown out candles on your birthday cake and made a wish, you have done an Affirmation! It is as simple as that!

Any Affirmation declared with conviction and belief manifests that which it affirms. When you do an Affirmation, you transfer a portion of your life force to that Affirmation and create a magnetic flow of energy. When you affirm, you express the desired experience by way of positive statements. What you genuinely want is already in the area of your subconscious mind. A strong desire for something starts it flowing toward you.

When used properly, Affirmations are powerful psychological tools for growth. Some people refer to the Affirmation process as 'treasure mapping,' or 'creating a wish list.' Affirmations can also be referred to as magic wands or trigger tools. To produce the desired results, Affirmations must be done repeatedly, with commitment, faith, expectancy, and enthusiasm. This exerts a powerful impact on your belief system, emotions, health, and life. Because of your innate ability to co-create with God, the

Universe acts as a gigantic Affirmation machine, awaiting your orders.

What we think and do and say ripples out into the world. If you take a bowl of water and drop a small pebble into it, you can watch how the ripples go out from the area where the pebble was dropped. I like to do this with children so they can see this tangibly. Your words are like that pebble when dropped in, causing a ripple effect in your world and in the world of others.

Affirmations Are Natural

Whenever you are goal-setting with powerful, focused intent, you are actually doing a form of Affirmation. Whether or not you are conscious of doing Affirmations, it is a fact that you have done many in your lifetime. You may call it goal-setting, planning, wishing, or praying. Those of you who have experienced success with goal-setting will be absolutely thrilled with the incredible success you achieve when you do the Affirmation Process faithfully.

In the Bible, Jesus taught a form of Affirmation. He said, "Ask and ye shall receive, knock and the door will be opened, seek and ye shall find." These are affirmative, action-packed statements and clear indications of the power within us to make things happen in our lives.

5ᵗʰ **Creative Visualization**

4ᵗʰ **Affirmations**
3ʳᵈ **Mind Power**
2ⁿᵈ **Thoughts**

1ˢᵗ **Forgiveness**

The Five Building Blocks of the Affirmation Process

» Forgiveness and Releasing
» Thoughts
» Mind Power
» Affirmations
» Creative Visualization

I wanted to lay out these building blocks in order for you here, though they are described elsewhere in this book. We talked about thoughts, creative visualization, and the power of the mind. In this chapter, we are looking at the specifics about Affirmations. And in the other chapters you learn more about forgiveness and releasing and much more. Together these create a solid foundation upon which you build your dreams.

The Affirmation Process

The proper use of this Affirmation Process allows you to take control of your life using the five building blocks. This powerful process enables you to change your life as *you* decree.

To begin with, let's take a quick look at some of the different types of Affirmations you'll be learning about in this book.

Master Affirmations

Master Affirmations are your order to the Universe, describing exactly your definition of what you desire. They are also similar to goals.

Short Form Affirmations

Short Form Affirmations are made up of several *key* words taken from your Master Affirmation. They are a simple, easy, quick method of keeping your desires on the front burner of your mind.

Visual Affirmations

This is how you can get the attention of the subconscious mind. Create and draw on paper detailed pictures of what you want. Use color and make it specific, exciting and vibrant.

Writing Affirmations

This is where you write your Affirmations. You take them out of the *unknown* and place them in the *known*. You anchor them to the Universe by writing them on paper.

Speaking Affirmations

These are spoken, verbal Affirmations. This could also include singing, chanting, and/or whispering Affirmations. Never underestimate the power of a softy whispered Affirmation. Here you actually speak, chant or whisper these words out loud.

Thought Affirmations

These Affirmations involve thinking strongly about something you desire. Everything that exists was first a thought in someone's mind. That chair you are sitting on was first a thought in someone's mind!

Feeling Affirmations

Feel deep in your heart and body that what you desire has already been given to you. Then *Act as If* you already have what you are affirming for.

Action Affirmations

These Affirmations involve taking the appropriate action to prepare for the manifestation of your desire.

Planting Your Affirmation Garden in Five Steps

The five steps of the Affirmation Process are like planting a garden. The gardener carefully prepares both the soil and the seed. The method of doing Affirmations (creating the object of your desire) is the same process that takes place in the planting of a seed.

The Master Affirmation *is* the seed. The growing takes place in the darkness below the surface. When you finally see the results of your work blossoming, your garden becomes a living Affirmation of love and joy.

Step 1 — Seed Selection

Decide exactly what you desire. Be very specific

Step 2 — Soil Preparation

Clear the way through releasing, forgiveness, and living in an attitude of gratitude

Step 3 — Planting, Watering, and Fertilizing the Seed

Read your Master Affirmation. Write and speak your Short Form Affirmation. Use your five senses to create the subconscious mind's reality of having what you desire

Step 4 — Trusting That the Seed Will Grow

Continue to hold firm and securely the image of *what* you want to create, and allow God/Universal Mind/Creator/Higher Self to take care of the *how*.

Step 5 — Bringing In the Harvest

Bring in your five physical senses to assist you in blowing breath into your Master Affirmation. When opportunity knocks at your door, don't forget to open it! Take the appropriate action right away.

Following these five steps will be easy once it becomes clear to you that you are collaborating with God/Universal Mind/Creator/Higher Self. You are not doing this alone! You are in fact a part of a great and powerful Team.

The Importance of Writing in the Affirmation Process

Writing formalizes the Affirmation process. When you write out an Affirmation, you are talking to yourself or thinking on paper. The moment you write out your Affirmation, it is on the way to happening for you. Written words are a step closer to the materialization of your Affirmation. When you write down a thought on paper, your full attention is automatically focused on it. The written word exists for all time.

By writing down your thoughts, you anchor them to the Universe and engrave them on your mind. Writing an Affirmation uses a larger part of the brain than mere thought and places your Affirmation in the area of reality, transforming the intangible into the tangible.

If You Want to Receive, You Need to Accept!

Total acceptance is a very important part of the Affirmation Process. To confirm your willingness to accept the outcome of your Affirmation, I encourage you to write on the bottom of the Master Affirmation, "I fully accept," and sign your name and address. Then fill in the date. A check is not valid unless it is dated and signed. Your Master Affirmation is a firm, binding document (contract) with yourself, your subconscious mind, and God/Universal Mind.

More on Master Affirmations

Supplies to Create Your Master Affirmation
- » Colored marking pens
- » Pad of Paper
- » Pen
- » Plastic Insert Sleeve (Sheet)
- » Picture of person and/or object desired
- » Glue or scotch tape

Sample Master Affirmation

Remember, for Affirmations to be truly effective you must appeal to your five senses, and the Affirmation must engender a positive, emotional state. Use words that trigger feeling and emotion in your body. Make your Master Affirmation colorful, because color wakes up and excites the subconscious mind. And placing a picture of what you are affirming for at the top of your Master Affirmation gives your subconscious mind something upon which to focus.

Sample Master Affirmation

(Picture or sketch of what you desire)

"I, (your name), deserve and now have (or I deserve and now am) _____

_____

(write whatever it is that you desire here, being very specific) _____

_____

_____

_____

_____

to the good of all parties concerned, I now release this request, with faith, to my subconscious mind, knowing that it has manifested. I give thanks to God for the perfect answer to my Affirmation/prayer. Thank you, thank you, thank you.

I fully accept

Signed _____

Dated _____

Address _____

Sample Short Form Affirmation: *My desire is now manifesting* (or several key words taken from your Master Affirmation)

You only need to create your Master Affirmation ONCE (like doing a will). Make it colorful and interesting so you will want to look at it often. Color wakes up and excites the subconscious mind. Place it in a plastic insert sheet to keep it clean.

Please write **ONE** Master Affirmation per page. This way it does not become confused. If you give the Universe a confused order, you receive a confused answer. Make it clear and very specific stating exactly what it is you are affirming.

It is most important *before* you create, read, or say your Affirmations that you experience the feeling of deep emotion – excitement, anticipation, faith, and expectancy in every cell of your body.

Read your Master Affirmation every morning and every evening.

The Affirmation Rules: A Vital Part of the Process

The information in this book is so powerful that it comes with a warning. It is so important to abide by the following Affirmation Rules for everyone's benefit, and that includes you!

The Affirmation Rules

- » Never hurt or take from anyone
- » All Master Affirmations must include the safety clause, *to the good of all parties* concerned
- » You need to have at least a 51% believability factor that your Affirmation can manifest as affirmed
- » Make all your Master Affirmations very specific, saying exactly what you desire

» All Master Affirmations must contain the 3 P's, positive description, personal words and be stated in the present tense
» All Master Affirmations need to be accepted, signed and dated
» 'Act As If' your Master Affirmation has already manifested as affirmed
» Say, "Thank you, thank you, thank you"
» Make your Master Affirmation colorful, exciting and interesting
» Feel that you really 'deserve' what you are affirming
» Oh yes, have fun!

Remember your Short Form Affirmation consists of several *key* words taken from your Master Affirmation, which can be jotted down on a piece of paper several times daily and repeated daily as many times as you wish. This process keeps your Affirmation on the front burner of your mind.

More About Including "To the Good of All Parties Concerned."

The 'Safety Clause'

This is one of the most important clauses in your Master Affirmation. You must use this clause in *every* Master Affirmation, because it is your safety net. When you say, *to the good of all parties concerned,* you eliminate the possibility of negative interference. Also, when you use this phrase, your Affirmations will not manifest unless they are to the good of everyone involved and this, of course, includes you!

You could also add to your Affirmation, "This or some-thing better now manifests for me." Think big and expect and enjoy delicious *Cosmic Affirmation Cookies* from the Universe!

$100,000 Lesson

I refer to the following story as my $100,000 lesson! On one occasion, when I was a party in a lawsuit, I affirmed that the judge would rule in our favor. I sat in the court-room staring at the judge, projecting this thought at him. I did this procedure for the entire duration of the trial. To everyone's surprise, the judge did rule in our favor and awarded us a sum of money. This led to my invest-ing additional money to open a restaurant in Ferndale, Washington—which turned out to be the worst possible thing that could have happened, in this instance. It caused me much worry, work, grief, heartache, and the loss of US $100,000.

I truly believe that, if I had added to my Affirmation the safety clause, *to the good of all parties concerned,* the judge would have decided differently, which would defi-nitely have been to my highest and best good. This was a very expensive, yet valuable, lesson.

Several years ago, one of my students did an Affirmation to receive money. She simply affirmed she had received the sum of $5000 to purchase an automobile. She went to a party, drank a little too much, and took a taxi home. She was in a car accident and was injured seriously enough to necessitate being off work for several months. Her settle-ment turned out to be $5000—right to the penny!

I asked if she had ended her Affirmation with the safety clause, *to the good of all parties concerned*, as I had taught her. She admitted to me that she had not.

If she had added this clause to her Affirmation for $5000, I feel sure she would have received the money in a different manner and been spared the injury. Her story is a good reminder of the utmost importance of adding to all your Affirmations, *to the good of all parties concerned*.

When teaching Affirmations, I am very careful to stress the importance of *always* adding this very essential clause.

More about Giving Thanks: Being Grateful in Advance

Be thankful. Adopt an attitude of gratitude. It is easy to give thanks *after* you have received your blessings. Give thanks *before*. Write "thank you" three times after *every* Master Affirmation. When you say "thank you," you obligate the planet to bring you more. Have and maintain an attitude of gratitude and watch miracles happen in your life.

One day, my daughter Aren told me of something she just *had* to do for someone, right then. She was insistent. When I asked her why, she said, "I have to, Mother. They thanked me in advance and now I feel so obligated."

Gratitude is the willingness to be thankful for what you have and a celebration of lessons learned from life's experiences. It is so important to live in an attitude of gratitude, and to focus on and be thankful for the good things that we have in our lives and for the good that is coming to us, rather than focusing on the things we are lacking.

More about the '3 P's'

It is important to follow this rule (just like all the other rules), as it truly can affect the outcome of your Affirmation.

» Make sure that you describe what you want to create using *positive* descriptive words, rather than describing what you *do not* want

» Keep your Affirmation *personal* by putting yourself into the wording of your Master Affirmation. "I, (your name), deserve and now have . . . "

» As stated earlier, it is important to always affirm in the *present time* because it is the only time frame in which the subconscious mind operates. If you say, "I, (your name) deserve and will have . . . " you are putting the manifestation of your Affirmation off into the future, perhaps some future lifetime!

When you use the 3-P Rule, you make your Master Affirmation positive, you make it yours and you expect it to take place immediately — that is in the present tense. This is a very powerful and unique combination which creates success!

More about Having Fun with Your Affirmations

Make your Affirmation Process FUN! You are creating something wonderful, something exciting and one of a kind. It is your own creation. Properly Done Affirmations are very powerful! Remember you can affirm and have anything in the world you desire as long as you adhere to the Affirmation Rules.

Let your mind run wild! Affirm for things you never thought possible. As long as you are careful to add the safety clause, you are protected. Remember that your sub-conscious mind does not know the difference between a real and an imagined event; it just obeys your conscious mind.

To Recap:

The conscious mind is like the captain of a ship who gives the orders and your subconscious mind is like the crew who obey the captain's orders immediately without question.

Every Journey Begins with the First Step

Every journey begins with the first step—one step at a time, one miracle at a time. Be aware that every goal or Affirmation consists of several steps, each one based on the previous one. The first step of any journey or program is of prime importance. Once the steps are clearly formed in your mind like a picture, they are easy to follow.

These steps are the Affirmation Process, the master plan that carries you to the materialization of your goals and Affirmations. Everything in life is like a progression of steps. If you swallowed a large apple whole, you would choke. If you cut the apple up into bite-size pieces and ate one piece at a time, you would accomplish the task of eating the apple. A baby first crawls, then walks, then runs. It is so important to do the first step, which is deciding what you really desire, then to do the appropriate Affirmation that produces the desired result.

For example, if you are affirming to become a lawyer, there are going to be many steps for you to take to manifest your goal. Tackle one task at a time, one step at a time, and one grain of sand at a time.

One of my students told me that her Affirmations were coming true in stages or baby-steps. I advised her to put Step One, Step Two, and Step Three on her Master

Affirmations and check off each step as it manifested for her. This is a faith-builder.

Be flexible. Change and revise your Affirmations as often as necessary. As you change, your Affirmations change. Make adjustments and allow room for the unexpected. Welcome new ideas and be self-disciplined and persistent. Perseverance means hanging in there when all the odds appear to be stacked against you.

Affirmations When Properly Done Always Work!

CHAPTER 3
APPLYING THE AFFIRMATION
PROCESS TO YOUR LIFE

Step 1--Seed Selection: What Do You Want in Your Life?

Clear your mind and put yourself in a positive, receptive mode. Go within and discover the most important things you want to attract into your life, whether it's a romantic relationship, a new job, abundant money for your children to go to university, a deep feeling of happiness, or whatever you desire.

Ask Yourself
   » What are my fondest dreams and wishes?
   » What would I like to see take place in my life?
     Really think about it.
   » How would I feel if I already had these things?

Now, without holding back in any way write down 3 things you would like most to manifest into your life. Take time to decide what you *really* want, being very specific — with absolutely no limits. If you aren't specific about what you want, you could be disappointed. Tailor it to suit your own true desire.

To make up your mind is a wondrous thing. It directs you toward your mental image and sets you on the path. *Decision* is an important part of everyday living. Every moment of every day, we are all making big and small decisions. When you decide to accomplish something, you mentally toughen yourself to make it happen.

To help you focus and get clear about what you want, ask yourself the following questions:

» Do I want it with all my heart?
» Is this merely what someone else wants for me?
» Do I have at least a 51% believability factor that it can manifest?
» Whose voice am I hearing?
» How do I really feel about it?

When you have the answers to these questions, you will know if you truly desire what you are affirming.

Remember:

Be *specific in the details that matter to you*. It is important to know the meaning and spirit of your Affirmations. Look up the meaning of any unfamiliar words you use in your Affirmation, to ensure that you use powerful, descriptive words that you totally understand.

For example, if you want a new car, you might state exactly what make and model you want, the color, type of tires, whether it is automatic or stick shift, if it has a state of the art stereo system, air-conditioning, radio, or power windows, etc. This is your order to the Universe and your job is to be precise in what you are asking for.

Make sure your heart and mind are in agreement with your Affirmation and that it resonates with you.

Write out what you desire in the form of a Master Affirmation, being sure to follow the five *Affirmation Rules* and to state everything in the present tense and in a positive way. Mentally plant the Master Affirmation (seed-thought) into the rich, fertile soil of your subconscious mind. The mind knows only to reproduce what is planted in it (what you are affirming). These words become your Master Affirmation — your order to the Universe.

Sample Master Affirmation for a New Car
[picture of your desire]

"I, (your name), deserve and now have the perfect, most wonderful brand new car for me, and the money to maintain it well. It is easy to drive and easy to maintain. It is a silver four-door automatic with plenty of room for the whole family and our luggage, too. It has air-conditioning, power windows, a GPS system, and a great radio/CD player/sound system. It is very comfortable and is absolutely safe for all of us, always. It is a joy to drive. I am healthy, happy, and love my new car. To the good of all parties concerned. Thank you, thank you, thank you!

I fully accept"

Signed_____

Dated_____

Sample Short Form Affirmation: Brand new car for my family and me

Once you decide exactly what you desire, it can be a stretch between what you have chosen and what you believe is possible. Step 2 can take you closer.

Step 2—Soil Preparation: Clearing the Way with Forgiveness and Gratitude

Prepare the soil of your subconscious mind by forgiving and releasing everyone and everything that has ever hurt you. Then forgive yourself. The forgiveness exercises can be done by physically writing them, saying them out loud, or visualizing them in your mind. Once you have done this, the freshly prepared soil of your subconscious mind is ready to receive the seeds.

Forgiveness heals even the deepest of wounds. It is very powerful. When you forgive, your energy changes the physical structure of your cells and DNA. When you are embroiled in guilt, shame, or depression, you close down the energy systems of your body. All types of negative problems can erupt.

When you come across a 'wound,' say to yourself: "I, (your name), now forgive everyone and everything that has *Ever* hurt me. I now forgive myself. I love, respect, and approve of myself just the way I am."

Note: When you say *Ever* it goes right back to creation—to when you were in your mother's womb, so if too many memories surface at the same time, just say "One at a time please."

Forgiveness is a choice, as is *not forgiving*. When you *do not* forgive another person, you remain energetically connected or tied to them. When you forgive others, you break those ties and allow them to move on with their lives—and you to move on with yours.

And so, forgiveness is a process of untangling mental and emotional parts of your being. If you have become tangled up in the negative energy of another person or situation and need to forgive, you will learn now how to use the power of forgiveness to heal yourself and get rid of negative people, conditions, thoughts, ideas, and concepts. And give yourself permission and credit for being capable of changing negative feelings about yourself, your life, and the past. When you stop blaming others, wishing things were different, or judging something to be wrong, you *can* truly forgive yourself and others.

Gratitude is advanced forgiveness; it is therefore also important to *be grateful* for your blessings.

The next chapter is devoted to the issue of Forgiving and Releasing. In it you will find more exercises and suggestions to help you with this step in your Affirmation Process.

Step 3—Planting, Watering, and Fertilizing the Seed Caring For Your Affirmation Every Morning and Evening

Once you've written out your Master Affirmation you are at the point of no return (although you can always choose to pass up the opportunity). You have told the Universe what you want, however, there may still be obstacles in your path.

Forgiveness and gratitude help to narrow the gap between what you've chosen to create and what you believe is possible. Now it's time to make it a reality. And you have the tools:

Read your Master Affirmation every morning and evening. Write out your Short Form Affirmation seven times every morning and evening (you can either keep this paper or dispose of it). Say it out loud. Now use your five senses to create your subconscious mind's reality of having what you desire. Creative visualization is the way to do this.

Visualize in your mind your desires, creating vivid pictures and making them crystal clear. Bring in the five physical senses. *See, hear, smell, taste,* and *feel* what you are affirming.

To use the example from Step 1, create vivid pictures of you driving your new car and enjoying every minute of it. The more detailed and colorful you make your mind pictures, the more you will be able to hold those pictures firmly in your mind until they manifest as affirmed. For example: **PICTURE** yourself going into the car dealership.

Bring in your 5 Physical Senses

SEE the sales person in vivid detail. Picture yourself signing the Car Purchase Agreement. Create the feeling of belief as the sales person places the car keys in your hands. Notice the excitement that is building inside of you.

FEEL the steering wheel in your hands as you drive your new car. Notice the feeling of happiness. What else do you feel? Now visualize yourself driving your new car into the countryside.

HEAR the motor purring. Are you alone? Do you have a passenger? Who is it? What are the road conditions? Is the sun shining? Are you excited?

SMELL the fresh country air. Inhale the soft, gentle breeze as it caresses your face and blows through your hair.

TASTE the fresh, pure country air, and whatever other delicious flavor you would like to imagine.

Listen to the sound of the motor purring.

You are creating a strong belief through feeling as if you already owned that most wonderful new car. The mind does not know the difference between a real and an imagined event, and accepts and stores the visualization as reality.

Your Ability To Believe IS What Matters!

When doing your Affirmations, you need at least a 51% believability factor that the Affirmation will manifest as affirmed. If you think about percentages in business terms, when you have 49%, someone else is in control, when you have 50%, it is stalemated, but when you have 51%, you have controlling interest!

You can increase your ability to believe that your Affirmation will come true by doing the following:

» Affix with scotch tape a tiny mustard seed to your Master Affirmation. Then look at it and know that when you only have the faith as big as that tiny seed, miracles happen!

» Say over and over, "I believe, I believe, I believe." Also say, "I KNOW what I am affirming is NOW manifesting for me."

» Meditate on feeling that you really and truly deserve and are entitled to what you desire.

» Use the *Borrow Back Technique*. Go back into your memory bank and recall all the things that you wished for really hard and you got them. Also recall a time when it was magical. You just thought of something and it arrived in your reality. Then build on this feeling.

» Listen to self-help tapes and read self-help books.

You must feel that you deserve what you are affirming. Sit and meditate and *feel* and know that you deserve to have what you desire!

Make your creative visualization pictures colorful and exciting. A specific, vivid, mental picture gives the subconscious mind something definite on which to focus. Remember, thinking in pictures is one of the basic activities of the human mind. The instant you visualize in vivid color the end result of your Affirmation, the energy and power of your visualization take the form of a tiny speck in your consciousness. It is your choice whether to leave it where it is, as it is, or to give it life to grow. Faith is the power and life force that fertilizes it. Faith, emotion, and expectancy fuel the imagination of the subconscious mind and make your Affirmations manifest more quickly.

The Importance of Focus: One Affirmation at a Time

If you hold a magnifying glass over a small portion of a newspaper, outdoors on a sunny day, the paper will burn if the sunlight is strong enough. This is an example of focused energy. Nothing will happen if you hold the magnifying glass at a distance from the newspaper or move it quickly back and forth, because you are scattering the energy and power.

It is the same with Affirmations. You can work on many Affirmations at one sitting, but you must deal with one Affirmation at a time, so that you do not scatter the power of the focus. Should you place several Affirmations on one page, it can become confusing and you may dilute and scatter your focus.

When you do an Affirmation, focus and concentrate on what you desire. The results will be powerful.

Step 4—Trusting That The Seed Will Grow: Your Affirmation Manifests as Affirmed!

This step is all about trust. Learn from the lowly seed – there is a time to plant; a time to take root and grow; and a time to bloom and become.

Because the Affirmation Process is collaboration between you and God, Universal Mind, Creator, Higher Self, or whomever you believe in, you don't need to worry about the modus operandi (the way it happens). You know the **What** that you want, and God, Universal Mind, Creator, Higher Self know the **How**. Your responsibility is to affirm, and then to wait for the answer to come to you, and finally, *to take action on it when it does.*

Continue to do *Step 3* every day. Continue to hold the image of what you want to create, and let the Affirmation process itself do the 'figuring out How.' God, Universal Mind, Creator, Higher Self takes care of it.

Know that you already have that which you are affirming for. It simply has not physically materialized yet!

Over-Attachment to the Outcome

There is a very important concept to consider -- about how strongly you attach yourself to the outcome you desire. Are you *overly* attached to what you want? If you spend too much time worrying about the modus operandi, or if you are too attached to what you want, then you actually *push it away* instead of attracting it.

Many people delay the completion of their desires by being rigidly attached to the *exact* outcome. When you are impatient, fret, worry, or feel too attached to the outcome of your Affirmation, you only hinder the process of manifestation. Affirmations can manifest in a different manner or time frame than expected. Release your completed Affirmations into the Universe with *loving detachment.* Assure your thoughts and Affirmations that they will find the perfect answer and return to you. *Bless* your Affirmations as you send them out into the Universe to manifest. You have now set free the mind power you activated. Your subconscious mind can then support the image and make the desire of your Affirmation a reality.

Cut the ropes of over attachment today, and allow and give your Affirmation permission to go out into the Universe, gather the required material and bring your Affirmation into manifestation right before your eyes!

Step 5 — Bringing In the Harvest: Taking Action and Receiving Your Desire

When opportunity is at your door, don't forget to open it! Take appropriate action right away.

When doing the Affirmation Process it is very important to keep in mind that most important part of the process 'blowing breath' into your Affirmation is taking the appropriate action right away.

Barb's Story

Barb was doing a Master Affirmation to attract that loving, lasting, happy relationship with the perfect man to her. She went to visit her mother at her summer home in Washington State. Her mother was having some work done on the sun deck, and the day before, one of the workmen hurt his finger and could not come to work so he sent his son to fill in for him. That was the day that Barb was visiting.

She looked out the window and saw Jeff (the son) and thought to herself, "Hmm he is cool!" So she made some coffee and muffins and invited him and his other helper in to share them with her and her mother. The conversation went very well, and it turned out that Jeff knew some people that Barb knew and just as he left, he turned to Barb and said, "Hey, how would you like to go for lunch next week?" Barb cleared her throat and said, "What day are you thinking about?" He replied, "I am off next Saturday night; will you be down here then?" So they went out for dinner, started dating and now they are married.

It is interesting to me that Barb said, "But Dr. Evers, I did not even have to leave the house or blow breath into my Affirmation!" I told her to hang on a second and go back in her mind and think about the chain of events. Did she blow breath into her Affirmations? You bet she did. She looked, liked what she saw and took the further action of baking muffins and then inviting him in for coffee. She also took the action of acting on his invitation for dinner and finally his offer of marriage. So you see she DID blow breath into her Affirmation which resulted in what she had been affirming for several months.

Totally accept the manifestation of your Affirmation. Take possession of it. Now is the time to express your gratitude saying, "Thank you, thank you, thank you for the completed result." You have now completed the fifth step and you are in possession of what you have been affirming (ordering up!). Feel the gratitude in every cell and every part of your body.

Live in an attitude of gratitude.

You deserve a medal! The work you have done is now paying off!

Enjoy your creation!

Keeping Track Along the Way

A good strategy is to start by affirming small things in the beginning, and then move on to larger things. I encourage you to keep a record of what you have achieved through your Affirmations. I recommend having a *Fulfilled Master Affirmation Book* that you can fill with numerous completed Affirmations – to remind you that this process works. By keeping track of your positive results with the smaller things, you will increase your faith to move on to new and larger goals. When even your smallest Affirmation manifests, you will experience a feeling of excitement and amazement.

Master Affirmation Checklist
- ☐ Is it specific, stating exactly what you desire?
- ☐ Is it heartfelt and emotionally charged and does it resonate with you?
- ☐ Do you feel it in your body?
- ☐ Did you release negative feelings and beliefs?
- ☐ Is your heart and mind in agreement with your Affirmation?
- ☐ Have you added the words 'deserve and now have?'
- ☐ Is it colorful, exciting, and interesting?
- ☐ Is it designed not to hurt or take from anyone?
- ☐ Is it *to the good of all parties concerned*?
- ☐ Is there at least a 51% believability factor that the Affirmation can manifest?

☐ Did you say *Thank You* three times? When you do this, you obligate the planet for more.

☐ Is it dated?

☐ Is your acceptance statement signed?

☐ Did you say YES to the Universe?

☐ Did you have fun?

If you answered yes to all the above questions, congratulations! You have just completed your first Master Affirmation!

Affirmations When Properly Done Always Work!

CHAPTER 4
WHAT'S IN THE WAY?

Under Step 1 of the Affirmation Process, we suggested to mentally plant the Master Affirmation (seed-thought) into the rich, fertile soil of your subconscious mind. The mind knows only to reproduce what is planted in it (what you are affirming.) But what if your life's garden refuses to grow your desires because it's so full of weeds? Your subconscious mind will keep reproducing those weeds dutifully unless you pull them out.

Those weeds are old negative patterns, and they become obstacles on the path to your Affirmation's full manifestation. Removing old, negative beliefs and replacing them with positive ones is an essential part of creating what you want in life. Forgiving and Releasing make up one of the *5 Building Blocks* of the Affirmation Process.

You are made up of billions and billions of beliefs about your body, your material worth, God, sin, life, life after death, etc. You have taken on some of these beliefs from others, and have created some yourself, accepting them as the truth. When you hear an idea over and over and decide to adopt it as your own, it takes up residency in your belief system and becomes a part of that system. It is always there (and believe me, you can count on it to be there supporting you every step of the way), but is this the type of support you really want or deserve?

The good news is that you created that erroneous and negative belief and you have the power to 'uncreate' it.

You are the only decision-maker in your life and it is up to YOU to release old, stubborn, hindering blockages and clear the path for your Affirmation to manifest. Become aware that *NOT* having what you desire to manifest is only a state of mind. What is your state of mind?

How to Deal With the Weeds? Discover and Uncover

Step 1--Examine Your Beliefs

Spend some time searching out your own belief system as it relates to what you desire to manifest with your Affirmation.

Step 2--Discover and Uncover any Negative Blocks

Determine what is blocking you from attracting what you are affirming for into your life right here and right now. Go within yourself and find out the reasons you feel this way. Ask yourself if you are holding some erroneous beliefs.

Step 3--Clear Those Blocks Out!

Use the *Forgiveness and Releasing* tools in the next chapter to release the negative beliefs that are in your way.

I would like to share one of my own stories with you as an example of how this "weeding process." works.

My Story of Dandelions & Money

When I was struggling to make ends meet, I closed my eyes and affirmed/prayed for money, and a strange thing took place. Instead of seeing money or dollar signs, I saw fields and fields of dandelions. What in the world did dandelions have to do with my prosperity? What do you think dandelions, thoughts, self-esteem, and prosperity have in common? This is rather a strange combination, don't you think?

The sturdy dandelion plant has a unique way of blowing its seeds out into the Universe through a soft ball of dandelion fluff. Many of these seeds take root and grow, while others do not. My father passed away when I was sixteen and our family was very short of money. I finished high school early and worked two jobs to help feed our family. Dad had no life insurance.

In fact, my early diet consisted of dandelion soup, dandelion stew, fried dandelions, and dandelion salad. When I grew up I detested dandelions and yanked them out of the ground whenever I saw one. I seemed to get a kind of satisfaction by stomping them into the ground with my foot. Then one day much later, while I was pondering on things and wondering why I experienced a lack of money in my life, again my thoughts immediately went to the dandelions.

The seeds of the dandelions blew in the wind of time and settled in many areas of my life, my prosperity, my thoughts, my self-esteem and how I felt about money. How could I feel good about myself, as a child and now, when I had these thoughts?

Why doesn't my dad get a real job and stop preaching so he could afford to feed his family?

How could anyone like me when I wore funny, hand-me-down clothes?

Why do I have to work to help support the family?

Why can't we live like other people?

Why do I have to clean dog kennels to make money to feed our family? Isn't that my parents' job?

These thoughts and many other ones of low self-esteem and low self-worth had been blowing in the wind of time and, in some cases, taking root and growing. I was becoming poorer and poorer. I checked back to what I was thinking in my childhood. I immediately tuned in to these thoughts. I had thoughts that I could never amount to anything. I also felt that I did not have the right to be prosperous or happy because I was a poor preacher's daughter.

I processed these thoughts, images, and ideas as they came into my mind/consciousness. One by one, I started changing them to positive ones: We did not have a great deal of money at that time, but we did have a huge amount of love. That situation has absolutely nothing to do with me many years later. My parents did the best they could with what reserves they had at the time.

Then I put all the negative thoughts into a huge, pink balloon and sent it off into the Universe to be recycled into God's pure love. I really thought about my thoughts. I wrote them out and studied them. I was surprised at my reaction.

» Was it true my negative thinking was bringing poverty to me now?
» Was it true I thought I was unworthy and undeserving?
» Was it true these negative thoughts were affecting my self–esteem and keeping me poor and in a state of lack?

I discovered that all the answers to these questions were *yes!* Where did all this negative thinking originate?

I realized it originated within me. Everything is created within and nothing comes to us from without.

I needed to get to the base of operation where my negative thinking problem was and change it, in order to see changes take place in my life.

I picked a dandelion out of the garden (they were not hard to find) and studied it carefully. I looked at how beautifully it was formed and how perfect the flower was. As I wept, the block of ice around my heart began to melt. Then a feeling of love came over me, followed by forgiveness. I sat there and thanked that little dandelion and all its ancestors for the nourishment and food it had provided for me and my family during my childhood.

Then I forgave myself for hating dandelions and began to feel love pour from me into that little flower. It was a rather strange situation, but I lovingly placed that little flower in the flower box. It had no roots, but it lived for several weeks.

Every time I looked at it, I sent it unconditional love. Some very interesting things began happening in my life. I began to feel better about myself and I started to love, respect, and approve of myself just the way I was. I started to make much more money than I ever had in my life and, more importantly, money started going further. To this day I still thank that little dandelion and its ancestors for nourishment and especially for the lesson of financial prosperity and my self-esteem improvement. Without learning this valuable lesson, I would not have had the money to write my books, tapes, videos, cards, workbooks, etc. I say, "Thank you, thank you, thank you."

Today I can honestly say I love and appreciate dandelions for the good value, nutrients, and beauty they give us. Now instead of stomping dandelions to death, I bless them, blow them a kiss, and thank them. My self-esteem has greatly improved; I watch my thoughts, words, and self-talk. My prosperity has multiplied and I daily affirm and creatively visualize health, happiness, loving relationships, and prosperity for my family and myself.

So now you see how dandelions, thoughts, self-esteem, and prosperity were all in the same package for me and see how old, negative patterns can become so ingrained in your consciousness, it may be necessary to do some exercises to rid yourself of them.

Star Poem
Bite off more than you can chew
Then chew it!
Plan for way more than you can do
Then do it!
Attach your Affirmation
To a Star
Hold on Tight
And There You Are!

Affirmations When Properly Done Always Work!

Part 2

AFFIRMATION TOOLS

I have listed over 150 different Affirmation Tools for you to use whenever necessary in your life.

Use them wisely and live in an attitude of gratitude for this powerful information from God, Creator, Higher Self, Universal Mind, Divine Being, or whomever you believe in.

SOME OF MY FAVORITE AFFIRMATION TOOLS

My many hard copy Affirmation Books, Cards of Life AND these 8 Affirmation Tools are some of my favorites and ones that I use almost daily. I have added them in more than one section of this book.

1% Solution

One of my colleagues, Terry McBride, shared with me the following story. He said, "Dr. Anne Marie it is hard, if not downright impossible, to be lying in a hospital bed in excruciating pain saying, I am 100% healthy. I just could not do it as the gap was too big. So I devised a plan as follows." I said, "I am 1% better (or healthier) today than I was yesterday." He repeated this statement with faith, passion, belief and expectancy daily. Now he IS 100% healthy and doing workshops teaching other people the power of the Affirmation Process.

You see, his mind COULD and DID believe the 1% as it was believable and immediately set out creating conditions in his body for his optimum health. Using his method, you could say, "Today I am 1% closer to having all my bills paid, meeting that special person, having more money, etc." Do like Terry did and repeat this statement over and over every single day with faith, passion, belief and expectancy. Then, in 90 days, you will be 90% closer and in 100 days you manifest your desire.

4 Little Words

Years ago, I had a favorite hair stylist that was quick to 'fly off the handle' and become very angry without any warning. One day he asked me what he could do. I explained to him that I thought he was dealing with some issues that he had 'swallowed,' you know the ones that become what I call 'Internal Boils,' which have a way of erupting when we least expect it. So we did some forgiveness exercises and the next time I visited him, he had a huge sign on his mirror that read, "I am handling it!" This process worked wonders for him!

10 Magic Words That Changed Her Life

When Deanna came to see me she was very unhappy. She was desperate to find out how to become popular, especially as she had no dates and her friends were always dating. I thought about it and then I remembered a situation in my life. I was acting as a journalist and was asked to write a story on a very busy, famous millionaire. When I arrived at his office he said very firmly, "I only have 15 minutes to give you and then I have an important meeting." I agreed and we got started.

I asked him all about himself. I said, "Peter you are so interesting, please tell me about yourself." Well he did!

And one hour and a half later, I stood up and said, "Excuse me Peter, but I do have another appointment." I thought about this later and wondered to myself why he made such a point of telling me about the 15 minute time period and then gave me an hour and a half. Then it dawned on me! Of course, he was talking about the most important person in his Universe (him) and on that there was no time limit! I shared this story with Deanna and her eyes sparkled as she left my office. Did it work? Of course it did, and now she has so many dates her friends are asking her what her secret is?

21 Day Agreement

When making agreements, Affirmations, listening to tapes, etc. we always encourage you to do it for a minimum of 21 days as studies have shown that it takes 21 days to make a habit.

Percentage (%)

I use this process all the time. When I am writing my book, articles, columns, and writings, I calculate that I am __% finished. This really helps me stay focused as I know I am making progress. Try it, and see how it works for you.

10 Second Silence Magic

When you are negotiating a business transaction or are in a heated discussion with another person, this 10 Second Silence Magic is very important. I have saved many real estate transactions by asking a question, and then keeping quiet for at least 10 seconds. I count slowly 101, 102, 103, etc. It is known that people do not like silence, and they will break it, and you then can discover what their real objection or feeling is. It works in relationship disagreements as well, since it gives YOU that 10 second time to cool off and regroup your thoughts, words, and actions.

This Too Shall Pass

This is a very important and helpful exercise. I use it often and rely on it as one of my wonderful Affirmation Tools. When I am in an uncomfortable and/or negative situation, I simply visualize on the back of my ring these four words, 'This too shall pass,' and it does together with the good times. This is what we call life. I really see in my mind's eye these 4 words and receive power and comfort from them.

Hourglass

When I am overwhelmed, thinking "How can I ever get everything done that I need to do today?" I do the Hourglass Exercise. I have an hourglass on my desk close to my computer. I watch each grain of sand going through the tiny neck of the hourglass and think about how just one grain of sand is able to get through at a time. If I try to force more than one grain, it clogs up and stops. I use this in my life, doing only one task at one time and, that way everything gets done.
Remember:

If you swallowed a large apple whole, you would choke. If you cut the apple up into bite-size pieces and ate one at a time, you would accomplish the task of eating the apple. A baby first crawls, walks, then runs. It is so important to do the first step, which is deciding what you really desire, then to do the appropriate Affirmation that produces the desired result. Don't try to tackle the whole job at once!

Affirmations When Properly Done Always Work!
(sometimes not in our time frame or as we think they should)

Now let's get on with the Career Affirmation Tools!

CAREER AFFIRMATION TOOLS

10 Second Silence Magic

When you are negotiating a business transaction or are in a heated discussion with another person, this 10 Second Silence Magic is very important. I have saved many real estate transactions by asking a question, and then keeping quiet for at least 10 seconds. I count slowly 101, 102, 103, etc.

It is known that people do not like silence, and they will 'jump in' to fill it with words. Then you can discover what their real objection or feeling is. It works in relationship disagreements and other situations as well, since it gives YOU that 10 second time to cool off and regroup your thoughts, words, and actions.

This exercise is very helpful to use during the interview, Career Evaluation, the raise, and just every time you wish to find out what the other person is really thinking.

Interview -- Day before the Interview

Dress comfortably in a business-like manner.
Be neat, tidy and polite.

Use a Creative Visualization Exercise

Mentally visualize—in vivid Technicolor—exactly how you wish the interview to progress.
Bring the five senses into your creative visualization.
See your interviewer (just a rough sketch is fine).
Hear   him or her saying, "(Your name), I am so pleased to say I have scheduled you for a

second interview with the president. This is just a formality. You have the position."

Feel	the joy and pride at being selected for the position.
Smell	some cologne, flowers, or perfume.
Taste	a tangy mint.

Then step ahead, in your mind, two to three weeks or months and picture yourself in that career. Be certain to put yourself in the picture.

Before the appointment, find out all you can about the company and, if possible, the person who will be interviewing you. If your prospective interviewer is a golfer, speak about golfing. If he or she likes to fish, talk about fishing, etc.

Talk about the other person's interest; make the person feel he or she is the most important person in the world at that moment.

Interview Day –Role Play with Yourself

Transport yourself into the future, setting the scene up in your mind.

» Stay calm
» Do not allow yourself to become desperate or overanxious
» Be punctual, neat, clean, and well dressed
» Be confident
» Shake hands firmly
» Make frequent eye contact with the interviewer
» Smile and be yourself
» Speak clearly and professionally and avoid using slang

» Never speak negatively about previous employers or divulge trade secrets
» Employers like and appreciate people who are interesting, relaxed, competent, and willing to learn
» Show your prospective employers you are sincerely interested in working with their company
» Practise empathetic listening. Really *hear* what the interviewer is saying
» Respect the opinions of the interviewer and make comments, when appropriate
» It is nice to be important, but it is far more important to be nice
» Concentrate on what you have learned from previous work experiences
» Refrain from acting like a know-it-all

Career Evaluation

When you are about to be evaluated, do the following exercise. Creatively visualize in your mind's eye the office and person who will be evaluating you and your work. Make it very specific, bringing in your five physical senses.

Once you have the picture clearly in your mind, the office, furnishings, what is on the desk or table, your employer(s)?

What is he or she wearing?

Does he or she look frustrated?

What energy are you picking up?

Now it is up to you to set the scene the way you wish it to be. Remember your subconscious mind does not know the difference between a real and an imagined event. Let's start setting the scene.

» Really listen to the comments, concentrating on each word and letting them penetrate your mind
» Evaluate what the other person is saying
» Appreciate and value the good comments
» Give genuine thanks for praise
» Welcome constructive criticism
» Ask for clarification (ensure you understand the statements fully)
» Make suggestions on how to solve problems
» When applicable, say *No* nicely, with assurance
» Speak up for yourself
» Refuse to be labelled; do not accept unjust, unfair criticism of your work

Raise - Setting the Scene

Create the scene in your mind. Know that what you are asking for is realistic with the company profits, economy, etc. How do you feel about asking for a raise? If you are unhappy with the way you feel, create a new state of consciousness. Know with great certainty that you really are worth that much more money. Then create the mind picture in great detail.

» Have the amount you are asking for clearly fixed in your mind
» Know you are worth every penny
» Know that the company CAN afford to pay you more
» Be confident

Challenges with Employers and/or Co-workers

Uncover and Discover Exercise (Going within)

You may not be able to secure another new position until you have learned how to deal with a particular difficult person or situation at your present place of employment. The workplace is comprised of many varied personalities. It is possible to have a personality conflict with one of your co-workers, employer, or others. If this happens take steps to mitigate, improve and/or dissolve it.

Ask Yourself
» Are you expecting too much of your present career, company, or superiors?
» Could you be comparing yourself to fellow employees or competing with them?
» Do you feel you are being treated unjustly?

If this is the case, get to the root of the problem, examine it, discuss it, and then solve it.

» Are you being overly sensitive?
» Is there a legitimate reason for this treatment?
» Why do you feel it is unfair?
» Are you being passed over for promotions?
» Are you attracting this type of treatment by your attitude or actions?
» Does your attitude need to be adjusted or changed?

When you get the answers to these questions, you will be better equipped to look within, at the internal problem.

If you are satisfied with your answers and you have been honest, it may be time to secure another position.

Spiritual Disinfectant Exercise
On a piece of masking tape, write the words Spiritual Disinfectant. Place the tape on a small spray bottle.

Fill the bottle with water and, if you wish, add a drop or two of your favourite essential oil or perfume. When you encounter a negative situation, simply spray the air with the spray bottle, saying, "I now spray all negative thoughts and situations." You can also use this technique to spray away the negative thoughts of others. (Note: Never spray a person in the face.)

Tom goes to his office early each day and sprays around his work area before the other employees arrive. He is careful to avoid contact with the papers and materials in that area. He says he really notices the difference that activity makes in his day. Now co-workers comment that when Tom is absent, things do not run as smoothly in his department. He is convinced this spray method works very effectively.

One reader relates how she uses her Spiritual Disinfectant when her husband Greg comes home from work in a negative mood. When he goes into the kitchen, she gets out her Spiritual Disinfectant and sprays around his chair. She swears that 10 minutes later, he is back to his normal, positive self. Greg is totally unaware of this exercise. She is so excited about her wonderful results that she tells all her friends about her success.

Home Based Business
» Discover what career you feel passionate about
» Do some research on your subject of interest
» How many people are doing the same type of work?
» Check out the areas they are working in
» Check out opportunities on the Internet
» Write out a plan (your blueprint)
» Come up with your own idea and then brainstorm it with people you trust

» Do your homework by reading some of the numerous books available on setting up a home business
» Prepare a business plan to take to the financial institution for a loan, if required
» When you have your finances in place, start your business
» Be courageous
» Move forward even in the face of fear
» Talk to successful businesspeople
» Glean, modify, and utilize their good ideas
» Read success stories, books, attend self-help lectures, and listen to success tapes
» Pay yourself a salary, whether your business can afford it or not. Since time is money, it is also important to make wise use of your time and to keep your life and business orderly
» Organize your life and learn to delegate
» Make your business serve you

Your key to starting and running a successful business is acquiring and using the prosperity consciousness.

Home Business Success Stories

One man discovered his friends were always asking him to locate certain car parts, which he did, through auto wreckers, scrap yards, ads, and associates. He provided this needed service to others, too, and it became a thriving business.

Several years ago, four young men rented a truck, bought some tires and equipment, and went to a part of the Alaska Highway that is famous for flat tires and blow-outs. They found a need and created their own successful business venture to fill that need. They now have expanded to handling car repairs and other services for motorists.

Getting Clients to Call / Connect

Thoughts are picked up and acted upon anywhere, anytime, and by anyone in the world. Distance is no barrier. Consequently, you can think about--and concentrate on a certain person and cause him or her to contact you. You may already have had the experience of thinking or speaking about a person and then having him or her call or contact you.

When you need to contact a client to buy your product or services, do the following exercise.

Sit down, close your eyes gently, clear your mind, and take three deep breaths. On the 'in' breath, breathe in clarity and focus on your client purchasing your product/service. Be sure and add the safety clause, 'to the good of all parties concerned.' On the 'out' breath, exhale all doubt and negativity you may have about the client not purchasing, or you not receiving great wealth. Focus all your thoughts on receiving money in avalanches of abundance. Recall everything you can about your client.

Say loudly and clearly three times:

"(Name of person), this is (your name). I need to speak with you. It is very important. Please call. Thank you, thank you, thank you for calling me now to the good of all parties concerned."

Be certain to add the safety clause 'to the good of all parties concerned.' Then bring in your 5 physical senses

SEE that person clearly in your mind's eye

HEAR that person saying, "Hello this is (name of person); I had the strong feeling that I needed to call you"

FEEL   how happy you are that he or she is calling you

SMELL   their perfume or cologne

TASTE   a juicy grape, cherry, or tasty mint in your mouth

Whenever the image of that person flashes into your mind, say silently to yourself, "Thank you for calling me." I often use this simple method, with immediate and startling results.

Sample Master Affirmation for Career

"I, (your name) deserve and now have the perfect, successful, lasting career for me. I receive in excess of $ _____ monthly (net or gross). My employers and/or Company are happy with my wonderful, creative work and reward me accordingly with regular raises and/or bonuses. I enjoy harmonious working conditions. I am happy and fulfilled in my career to the good of all parties concerned. Thank you, thank you, thank you.

I fully accept"

Signed _____

Dated _____

Address _____

Affirmations When Properly Done Always Work!

CHILDREN AFFIRMATION TOOLS

Affirmation Tools to Help Your Children
Introduction to the Affirmation Process

Teaching your children to use the power of Affirmations at a young age is one of the best gifts you can ever give them. Although we start life with simple, childlike faith, we become programmed by limited, negative thinking. By making positive, affirming statements to your children, you program and encourage them in a positive way, enhancing their self-esteem and their faith in themselves.

Introducing Affirmations to Children

A simple method of introducing Affirmations to your children is to ask them to identify some personal goals or challenges in their life. These could be making friends, being accepted, being popular, liking school, liking teachers, or getting good grades. Reflect the child's feelings back to him or her.

Acknowledge, validate and understand your child's feelings and thoughts about the word Affirmations. Ask him or her what they think an Affirmation is and then give them the following simple explanation.

Simple Explanation

When he or she has a birthday cake, blows out the candles and makes a wish tell them they are actually doing an Affirmation.

Help your child formulate an empowering Affirmation that they are interested in. Keep is simple and make it fun in a positive self-statement, written in the first person, that the child can understand and say to him or herself.

The earlier you begin teaching your children Affirmations, the sooner you see positive results. Never *force* children to do Affirmations. Make it an exciting, imaginative journey or fun-filled adventure.

Affirmation Light Bulb for Family

You may wish to do your family Affirmations in a special place, such as a garden, meadow, arbour, or anywhere you and your family feel comfortable and at peace. I enjoy doing my Affirmation Program in my own mental Affirmation Light Bulb which helps make my Affirmations more focused and powerful.

To do this, visualize a huge, giant light bulb in front of you. Make it large enough for your whole family to step inside. It is complete with door and handle. Open the glass door and go inside. You can see through it in all directions. Just inside the door, there is a panel of push buttons.

When you are working creating harmonious family relationships and situations press the pink button. This color will then fill your Affirmation Light Bulb, penetrating the atmosphere and enabling everyone to breathe in the power of that specific color. When doing an Affirmation for money for a family vacation use the color green as green represents money and abundance.

Imagine putting your Family Affirmation into a soft, golden cloud and letting it float up and out the large fresh air vent at the top of the Affirmation Light Bulb. Release it with loving kindness and detachment into the Universe, to manifest as desired.

Now mentally harden the material around the bulb so that no one else can come in for this time.

Bring in the 5 physical senses.

SEE	a huge wicker chair, covered with large colored pillows in gorgeous pastel colors.
HEAR	soothing music.
FEEL	sit down in the chair—feel your body sink into deep relaxation.
SMELL	the sweet fragrance of roses.
TASTE	*pop a* mint into your mouth to complete the experience of the 5 senses.

I use this valuable exercise for a positive pick-me-up whenever I begin to feel discouraged or disheartened. I also sit, meditate, and ask for new, fresh ideas. When you do the Affirmation Process in this wonderful space, it helps solidify, clarify, and empower your Affirmations.

You can also imagine yourself within the Affirmation Light Bulb when you are in the company of negative people or circumstances.

Have fun! You can invite your whole family to participate in the Mental Family Affirmation Light Bulb exercise, making it an exciting learning experience for everyone. Allow each person to provide input and ideas so everyone feels involved. This is a very powerful exercise for families, helping them to communicate and interact more effectively and lovingly. The family that affirms, visualizes, and creates together *stays* together.

Here is an email that I received about the Affirmation Light Bulb Affirmation Tool!

Family Uses the Affirmation Light Bulb Affirmation Tool with much Success

Dear Dr. Evers,

Just wanted to let you know how much fun we had with the Affirmation Light Bulb Affirmation Tool you shared with us on one of your Radio shows. We decided to do it for our family--that is my husband Dan and I and our two twin boys. They are almost 10.

First of all, we had a family meeting and decided who was going to do what. We created this strange look-ing light bulb in our backyard. It was made from can-vass, cardboard and other materials. We found a bunch of lights and put them on a board to make a light panel. Then we took some chairs and mats and all went into the Affirmation Light Bulb. We laughed as we all looked so ridiculous but we were having so much fun as a family.

Then Bobby said to his brother Tommy, "What button do you think we should push?" Tommy said, "Let's push the green one for Go." So they did and then we all visual-ized a beautiful green color filling the Affirmation Light Bulb. We then did a family Affirmation to keep our planet green. Then I said, "Boys, what about pink for love?" They all agreed and then we did that one and we made it up as we went. We also did a family Affirmation for Love and Peace in the world. Talk about fun and excitement! We are discovering new ways to use the Affirmation Light Bulb and we will keep you informed. Great for building a sound family foundation. Way to go, Doctor. We love you."

Sibella, Wade, Bobby and Tommy, United Family from Spokane, WA.

Dear Affirmation Light Bulb Family,

Thank you for your wonderful and inspiring email. Please keep up the good work and I am delighted to hear about your family Affirmation Light Bulb Project success.

With love and Affirmation Blessings

Dr. Anne Marie Evers

Empathy Shoes

I like to use this exercise with children. I have an old pair of very large shoes. I decorate them with sequins, gold, happy faces, and images from the Cards of Life. When I am not happy with a person, I visualize in my mind that these shoes belong to that person. Then I slip them on over my own shoes and walk around for a few minutes, getting the feeling of what it feels like to 'walk in another's shoes.' This really does help me see that person and/or situation in a different, new, and more positive light.

One method that we used for our 3rd Grade Class in Washington State was the Empathy Shoes Process. We had the children bring old (as large as possible) shoes from home. Each child decorated their pair of shoes whatever way they chose. They had so much fun and some of the creations were rather outlandish. First of all I would explain the word empathy to them. Empathy means being sympathetic or having compassion for another and also to have the power of understanding and imaginatively entering into another person's feelings.

When your children start to bicker and fight amongst themselves, have them put on each other's Empathy Shoes and walk around in them pretending that they are for a few minutes, that other person and tapping into their feelings.

Dear Dr. Evers,

I have been listening with great interest about your Affirmation Tools that you talk about on your radio shows, and I must admit that I have used many of them with good success. Now I am wondering if you have any that you can share with us with regard to children, especially to help them respect one another. My three children, 9, 10 and 13 seem to always find something to fight about and it makes for a chaotic time in our home. I appreciate the fabulous work you are doing in sharing these wonderful principles, Affirmations and tools with us. *Betty, Teacher, Marysville, WA*

Family Affirmation Method

Children who do Affirmations on a regular basis are more independent and responsible and they experience greater self-confidence and self-esteem. It is easier for them to know what they want and achieve their goals, desires, and wishes. They are able to say *No* more easily to negative situations and people. They attract, develop, and enjoy greater optimism for the present and future.

Fear Dragon

Fear can be a block that keeps you from doing something you wish to do. For example, a fear of flying could prevent you from experiencing many wonderful travelling experiences.

Imagine your fear in front of you; see it in the form of a *fear dragon*. How big is it? What color is it? What shape is it? How close is it? Can you feel its breath? How hot is it? Do you feel uncomfortable? Now *mentally* take a club and place it in one of your hands and push the *fear dragon* away from you. You do not wish to *burn* yourself. You are stronger than any *fear dragon*.

Ask it to speak to you. Say, "Have you anything to say to me?" Listen with your inner ear. Now be firm with the *fear dragon*. Inform it that it has no place in your body or around you and that it has to go. If the *fear dragon* tries to hang around, say again, "You must go. You are not welcome in or around my being." Say, "Fear dragon, you have no power over me. You are helpless. I am the powerful force here and you must obey me. I am the boss." Be firm and the *fear dragon* will vanish completely. Now, in its place, create an image of what you wish to accomplish.

For example, see yourself on an airplane embarking on some exciting adventure. See yourself surrounded by a pink, soft bubble—being safe and content, enjoying the flight to wherever you desire. This technique is very effective in banishing any limiting fears, and helping you achieve what you want.

Fear Zoo Exercise

You might wish to put your fears into proper perspective by forming your own fear zoo—a place where you can put all your fears. You may fear a wild tiger in the jungle but would you fear a tiger in a cage in a zoo? My own Fear Zoo is where I place all my fears.

I visualize my fear of closed-in spaces as a ferocious tiger, my fear of rejection as an angry gorilla, and my fear of failing as a giant giraffe. I visualize my fear of poverty and lack as two grizzly bears and any other smaller fears as cantankerous, quarrelsome monkeys. I visit them as often as possible. I look forward to our conversations and discussions! I consider them great, valuable teachers and learn from my experiences with them.

At times, I just sit quietly among them, feeling their presence and allowing them to feel and experience my presence. When you give fear a name and form and speak directly to it, its hold over you is lessened and its power is scattered.

What is your greatest fear? Name it, give it form, and speak directly to it in a controlled, safe atmosphere.

What animals will you choose? Your fear becomes manageable when you do this exercise.

One 3rd grade student visualized her fear of heights as a huge giraffe. After doing this exercise, she discovered to her absolute delight that her intense fear of heights had completely vanished.

Mirror Exercise

Look into the mirror and say, "Hey Self, you are a mighty fine person. I love, respect and approve of you. I let go of my negative, unhappy thoughts and replace them with happy, positive thoughts."

Positive Affirmation Game

Print Short-Form Affirmations on small pieces of cardboard (small flashcards) and place them into a box on the kitchen table. Encourage your child or children to pick one card every morning. Ask him or her to repeat the Affirmation three times and then to turn that positive statement over to his or her mind to attract other positive thoughts.

Depending on the age of your children adjust this exercise to suit your individual family. You can ask him or her what those words mean to them.

Use vivid, brightly-colored cardboard for the Short-Form Affirmations, which included the following:

» I like school
» I get good grades
» I am honest
» I am popular
» My teacher likes me
» I have many friends
» I feel happy
» I am smart
» I am on time
» I like learning
» It is easy for me to learn

Add happy faces, hearts, stars, and stickers to make the cards more attractive to the children.

Potential Glasses

Cut out pattern of eye glasses from heavy construction paper.

Cut out circles that fit into the glasses from plastic transparencies.

Color plastic circles green with permanent felt pen.

Decorate rims of glasses with glitter, sparkles, stickers or color.

Glue circles onto glass rims.

Put on glasses and SEE the potential in yourself and others.

Looking through colored glasses helps identify potential in everything we see.

When I taught this method to a grade 3 class, it was the most popular as student put on these Potential Glasses and felt they had an extra tool to add to doing Affirmations. They had a lot of fun and it taught them the lesson that *things are not as they seem at times* and to see and visualize good things in their lives and in the lives of their classmates and others.

Ripple Effect

A Ripple Effect is when you do something and it ripples out like a ripple from throwing a rock in the water. When you think negative, unhappy thoughts, you send out negative, unhappy thoughts to others and when you think happy positive thoughts you send those thoughts out to others.

Take a rock and drop it into a bowl repeatedly so that your child can see the ripples (rings) that spread out from the center of the water where the rock was dropped.

Count the ripples; compare the ripples in the water. When you do something unkind to another and he or she does the same to another, this is the ripple effect and this is how bullying starts.

How can we stop the ripple in the water or negative actions? The ripples in the water can be stopped by placing your hand into the water. Negative actions can be stopped by one of the kids refusing to carry on that negative behavior.

When I was teaching Affirmations to a 3rd grade class, Donald, the known class bully, said to me, "Dr. Evers, I used to fight a lot." I said, "Oh, you did?" With his hands on his hips, he replied, "Yep, but that was before I learned about Affirmations and the ripple effect."

Staying in Touch – Grown Up Lunch Exercise

Take your teenager (or younger) child out to a 'Grown Up Lunch' with just you (the mom or dad). Talk about your child's interest and then gently but firmly bring it around to discussing ways to improve your relationship. Let him or her talk about what is 'bugging' them and listen empathetically with both ears. Stop your mind chatter and concentrate and focus on the words you are hearing. Now write out an agreement setting out each person's expectations and establishing healthy boundaries. Both of you date and sign it; now you have made a firm and binding contract and a basis from which to work.

If the first or even second lunch is not too successful, keep on. Be persistent and slowly the emotional, negative walls start to crumble and then you can start the re-building process on a happy and positive note.

Eleanor's Story

Eleanor, a young mother of three — teenager Judy and two younger ones — is another inspiring example of how powerful a positive approach can be. Judy seemed full of anger and hate for her mother; Eleanor did not know what she had done to deserve this negative treatment. I helped Eleanor work out a plan whereby she would take Judy out for a grown-up lunch and they would each write gripe sheets about each other.

When lunch was over, they would enter into a discussion about how to improve their own relationship. They would talk out their hurts, emotions, and misunderstandings. They wrote an agreement setting out their expectations for each other and establishing healthy boundaries.

They both signed and dated it. Now they had a basis from which to work.

The first lunch did not go too well, but Eleanor persisted; the second lunch was very successful. Now both mother and daughter have a better understanding of each other. Eleanor says, "It is a miracle!" She realized the only person she could change was herself. She could and did, however, change the way she felt about and viewed her daughter.

If you expect respect, trust and love in return, treat your teenager and all your children with respect, trust, and love. You can still be that loving, caring parent while adding a whole new dimension — that of a trusted friend.

Don't worry about the small details. If you are sensitive and someone says hurtful things to you, simply say to yourself, "Cancel, cancel, I am happy." In this way, those hurtful statements will not be able to enter into your consciousness (your inner computer) and you will not have to deal with them.

Toothbrush Forgiveness Meditation

Parents

Please listen to this meditation first so you approve of the words. You can record this meditation for your child and encourage him or her to listen to it when you feel he or she needs a bit of encouragement or uplift. Help your child find a comfortable Place to sit so he or she will not be disturbed.

Ask him or her to gently close their eyes and take 3 deep breaths, breathing our fear and breathing in calmness and the feeling of being totally safe and taken care of.

Let's begin . . .

You are going on a totally cool, exciting and awesome journey within.

The Meditation

Today we are going to visit the School of Learning, about how to let go of past disappointments and hurts, and how to love, respect and approve of yourself. You will be going down 3 steps into total relaxation. At all times, you are safe and protected.

Focus on a body of water. Is it a bubbling brook, rushing creek, gigantic ocean, lake or river? Water represents life and emotions. Seeing this water relaxes you even further. Good – Now let's get started on today's meditation.

Step 1

Your body is a little numb and s-o-o relaxed you just don't feel like moving. You are so relaxed and peaceful.

Step 2

Going down deeper into total relaxation, still so safe and protected. Look, look, look over there. There is the School of Learning that you have heard so much about. You are getting very excited!

Step 3

You keep going down until you reach the bottom of Step 3. You see the sign that says 'School of Learning – Welcome, Come on In.'

Visualization--Seeing pictures in your mind. With your eyes still closed take some deep breaths breathing in and out 3 times.

Now it is very important that you really, really concentrate and focus on this Visualization.

You have arrived at the School of Learning and you are greeted very warmly by one of the teachers, Mr. White. He has a long white beard and piercing, yet kind eyes.

In your mind's eye--

SEE   the School of Learning

HEAR   the teacher, Mr. White, saying, "Hi and welcome"

SMELL   the scent of the fresh air

FEEL   how happy and absolutely thrilled you are

TASTE   biting into a juicy apple

Now focus on your visit at the school. As you enter one of the classrooms, you spot a huge oval mirror and by the mirror is a toothbrush and tube of toothpaste labeled 'Self-Esteem.'

Pick up the toothbrush, put some toothpaste on it and begin brushing your teeth while looking at yourself in the mirror. It is time to focus and concentrate very hard on your facial features, how great you look, how clear your eyes and complexion are, and your great, white teeth. Make it very real.

Then say, "I now let go of any and all feelings of fear, frustration or anger connected with me feeling good about myself. I am in complete control of my body right here and right now. I am the boss of my body. I love, respect and approve of myself just the way I am."

When brushing your teeth visualize in great detail how the brushing of your teeth is getting rid of any food particles and any other unwanted particles in your mouth area, just as you are getting rid of any tickling sensation in your nose and you are completely in control of all movement of your hands.

Put the toothbrush down and thank Mr. White at the School of Learning for providing you with the huge mirror, toothbrush and toothpaste to do your exercise.

Say, "Thank you, thank you, thank you," as you leave the School of Learning.

"Wow, is this ever cool," you say excitedly. "Now I see how brushing my teeth is like cleaning out all my negative thoughts."

Open your eyes, stretch and slowly return to the present moment. For a few moments, just relax and enjoy the feeling of pure happiness that flows throughout your body. You are completely healthy and in control of your body. With a huge smile on your face you start back up the steps to go home.

Step 3

You can taste the refreshing toothpaste and your teeth feel so squeaky clean.

Step 2

Going up further. Take a look back at the beautiful oval mirror and the mixed colors of the toothbrushes. Breathe in peace and relaxation. Know you can come back and visit any time you wish.

Step 1

You have arrived — back where you started from. You can't wait to get home and tell your family and friends about your awesome toothbrush experience.

Congratulations, you ARE very healthy and in control of your body. All negative fear has left your body, never to return.

Sample Master Affirmation for Children

"I, (your name) deserve and now have a loving, happy, healthy family. We have harmonious family relationships with each other. We give each other space to grow, become and be. We practice loving kindness with our family members and all others. We are all happy and fulfilled to the good of all parties concerned. Thank you, thank you, thank you.

I fully accept"

Signed _____

Dated _____

Address _____

Affirmations When Properly Done Always Work!

CREATION AFFIRMATION TOOLS

Use the information in my Affirmation Books to create your fondest and innermost dreams. Also go to the www. cardsoflife.com to receive answers to your questions about life.

21 Day Agreements

When making agreements, Affirmations, listening to tapes, etc. we always encourage you to do it for a minimum of 21 days as studies have shown that it takes 21 days to make a habit.

Abbreviation Short Form Affirmation x 77 Times

This is one of my favourite Affirmation tools which I use daily.

Write at the top of a page several words. Say you are affirming for health; write Abundant Health me now. Write it legibly and large enough that it is easy for you to see. Now below that sentence, jot down the abbreviation which would be the first letter of each word, (abbreviation) 77 times below the sentence. It is very important to say the words out loud as you do this exercise.

It may seem like a lot of work but it does not take long and it is well worth the effort. I can't tell you all the wonderful results I have received and am receiving from this one simple technique.

Affirmation Garden (5 Steps)

The 5 steps of the Affirmation Process are like planting a garden. The gardener carefully prepares both the soil and the seed. The method of doing Affirmations (creating the object of your desire) is the same process that takes place in the planting of a seed. The Master Affirmation *is* the seed. The growing takes place in the darkness below the surface. When you finally see the results of your work blossoming, your garden becomes a living Affirmation of love and joy.

Step 1 — Seed Selection
Decide exactly what you desire. Be very specific.

Step 2 — Soil Preparation
Clear the way through releasing, forgiveness, and gratitude.

Step 3 — Planting, Watering, and Fertilizing the Seed
Read your Master Affirmation. Write and speak your Short Form Affirmation. Use your five physical senses to create the subconscious mind's reality of having what you desire.

Step 4 — Trusting That the Seed Will Grow
Continue to hold the image of **WHAT** you want to create, and allow God/Universal Mind/ Creator/Higher Self to take care of the **HOW.**

Step 5 — Bringing In the Harvest
When opportunity is at your door, don't forget to open it! Blow breath into your Affirmation by taking the appropriate action right away.

Following these five steps will be easy once it becomes clear to you that you are collaborating with God/Universal Mind/Creator/Higher Self. You are not doing this alone!

Write Out Your Master Affirmation

The Importance of Writing in the Affirmation Process

Writing formalizes the Affirmation process. When you write out an Affirmation, you are talking to yourself or thinking on paper. The moment you write out your Affirmation, it is on the way to happening for you. Written words are a step closer to the materialization of your Affirmation. When you write down a thought on paper, your full attention is automatically focused on it. The written word exists for all time. By writing down your thoughts, you anchor them to the Universe and engrave them on your mind. Writing an Affirmation uses a larger part of the brain than mere thought and places your Affirmation in the area of reality, transforming the intangible into the tangible.

Date and Sign Your Master Affirmation

If You Want to Receive, You Need to Accept!

Total acceptance is a very important part of the Affirmation Process. To confirm your willingness to accept the outcome of your Affirmation, you could write on the bottom of the Master Affirmation, "I fully accept," and sign your name and fill in the date. A check is not valid unless it is dated and signed. Your Master Affirmation is a firm, binding document with yourself, your subconscious mind, and God/Universal Mind.

Learn From the Lowly Seed

This seed puts its roots and tiny tendrils down into the rich, fertile soil of the earth. It takes root and grows. At the same time, it sends sprouts up toward the light. When it encounters any obstacles, as it undoubtedly does, it is not discouraged. Instead, it simply goes around them, always stretching toward the life force of the sun and air.

The little seed shows no lack of faith, nor does it question the length of time it will take to manifest as a plant or tree. It simply acts, safe in the trust of God and the Laws of the great Universe. A seed of faith, once planted, never dies. The tiny seed is programmed. It puts all its energies into bringing its inherent blueprint into materialization. It knows, trusts, and acts. It produces without question, fear, or delay. Affirmations, like seeds, have a timetable of their own.

The process of doing Affirmations is a growing process. The knowledge of how to produce and create loving relationships, health, wealth, and happiness in your life was placed in you before you were born. This knowledge is activated through practising or doing properly done Affirmations.

If your thought, desire, or Affirmation arises at the instant when there are no conflicting thoughts present to nullify this power, the mind throws its great force behind that one desire or Affirmation. The power of the mind is not divided among other thoughts, so that particular Affirmation manifests immediately, as if by some form of magic.

Affirmation Light Bulb for Self

You may wish to do your *Personal Contract Affirmation Method* in a special place, such as a garden, meadow, tree house, arbour, or anywhere you feel comfortable and at peace. I enjoy doing my Affirmation Program in my own mental Affirmation Light Bulb, which helps make my Affirmations more focused and powerful.

To do this, visualize a huge, giant light bulb in front of you. Make it large enough to step inside. It is complete with door and handle. Open the glass door and go inside. You can see through it in all directions. Just inside the door, there is a panel of push buttons.

When you are working on the relationship Master Affirmation, press the pink button. For a career, press the green button—and for healing, press the blue button. The color you select will then fill your Affirmation Light Bulb, penetrating the atmosphere and enabling you to breathe in the power of that specific color.

Imagine putting your Affirmation in a soft, golden cloud and letting it float up and out the large fresh air vent at the top of the Affirmation Light Bulb. Release it with loving kindness and detachment into the Universe, to manifest as desired.

Now mentally harden the material around the bulb so that no one can come in or see you. Bring in the five senses.

SEE	a huge wicker chair, covered with large colored pillows in gorgeous pastel colors
HEAR	soothing music
FEEL	your body sinking into the chair
SMELL	the sweet fragrance of roses
TASTE	*pop a* mint into your mouth to complete the experience of the five senses

I use this valuable exercise for a positive pick-me-up whenever I begin to feel discouraged or disheartened. I also sit, meditate, and ask for new, fresh ideas. When you your Affirmation Program in this wonderful space, it helps solidify, clarify, and empower your Affirmations. You can also imagine yourself within the Affirmation Light Bulb when you are in the company of negative people or circumstances.

Create your very own peaceful place. It is a good idea to keep your own individual light-bulb space just for you. This is your secret place. Create whatever you desire. Make it special, unique, and completely safe. Allow your imagination and creative visualization abilities to run wild! Use it when required, but refrain from using it to avoid people who really do need your help and support.

Egg Shell

Placing your Affirmation/desire in an egg shell and putting it into the ground is like planting the seed of your desire. It acts as the seed from which your Affirmation takes root, grows and manifests in your life.

Write your desire or the amount of money you wish on a piece of paper. Cut it up into tiny pieces and place it in an empty egg shell. Put the top on the egg shell and then bury it in your back yard, or in a planter. This way you are grounding your Affirmation and giving it the conditions in which to grow and manifest.

Flashlight Exercise (Subliminal)

You may wish to try the following fun exercise. It works like the subliminal advertising that you see at hockey games, advertising Tim Horton's, RE/MAX, Toyota, etc. You sports fans are exposed to this subliminal advertising every time you watch a hockey game. While you are watching the game and the players, your subconscious mind is also taking in the strategically placed advertisements.

When you get hungry, your subconscious mind kicks in and says, "Yeah, let's go to Tim Horton's"; when you want to buy a new car it says, "Toyota"; to buy or sell real estate it says, "Call RE/MAX"; and for banking, "Call HSBC," etc.

I wonder how much money companies fork out for this type of advertising.

Flashlight Exercise

Write in big, green letters on a huge piece of chart paper the sum of money that you desire. Then write, "I am wealthy." Get up in the middle of the night and go into a dark room with all the lights off. Take a flashlight, aim it at the chart paper, and switch it off and on. Do this eight times, then go back to bed and immediately go to sleep.

Magic Genie Exercise

Think of your wondrous mind as your Magic Genie that is within you always, creating for you your fondest wishes. Be sure and give your Magic Genie (your subconscious mind) the proper instructions, being very specific.

Find a quiet spot, close your eyes gently, and visualize in vivid color and detail YOUR Magic Genie. See what he or she is wearing; see the facial expression, the eyes, hair, and every part of this Magic Genie. When your image is complete, thank this wonderful being for appearing and for making your wish come true. Ask for whatever it is that you desire, making it very specific. When you have finished, then say, "Thank you, thank you, thank you, my

Magic Genie, for granting my request," and say how very grateful you are.

Then open your eyes and go on about your day. Your Affirmation (wish) is already on its way to manifesting for you as you decreed.

Master Affirmation

This is your order to the Universe. Your statement of what you desire. Master Affirmations are very specific saying exactly what you desire to create in your life. Make certain what you are affirming for is what you and only you really want. Many of us want to please our loved ones and order up what we think they want for us. This is YOUR creation and create it as you wish.

Short Form Affirmation

This consists of several key words taken from your Master Affirmation. Short Form Affirmations can be jotted down three times on a scrap of paper and/or repeated over and over during the day. This Short Form Affirmation (SFA) keeps your request (Affirmation) on the front burner of your mind.

Meditation

Meditation is an effort made on the part of the conscious mind to close the gap between the Conscious and the Subconscious mind. Meditation is simply a quiet state of mind, a silence of thought. The growth of living things and the movement of the heavens are silent. The dictionary defines meditation 'to ponder or to engage in continuous and contemplative thought.'

It could also be described as thinking about doing something or planning to do it. Meditation is not daydreaming; it is surrendering, letting go, and sinking deep into relaxation. It is the attuning of the mental body and the spiritual body to its principal source—God. When you meditate, you empty yourself of everything that hinders your creative energies. Meditation sets the foundation for peace of mind and tranquility. In meditation, you learn to listen to your thoughts and create a space to *hear* your own voice. Pay close attention to what your mind is saying. Have a pen and paper close by so you can jot down any thoughts or insights that come to you when you still your mind.

Power of Words

Words are thoughts expressed. They carry the message and energy of your Affirmations with them. Some words are neutral, but most words are either negative or positive and charged with the emotion of fear or love. When you do word Affirmations, you speak the words out loud. Verbal Affirmations manifest what is affirmed by declaration. Every word filled with the positive emotions of faith and expectancy brings forth after its kind, in body, mind, and spirit. Whether shouted or whispered, your words have power. We create with every word we speak.

Never minimize the power of a softly whispered Affirmation filled with love and expectancy. You convey your innermost thoughts to others through language (words). Your words are powerful tools and have an energy all of their own. Words can convey love and cause peace and harmony between and among people and nations or they can convey hatred, creating wars and enemies.

Words are creative and you create with every word you speak. Affirmations convince the mind of the spoken and written word. Watch your words because they are very powerful. They have the power to injure or heal others. Keep track of the words you use in everyday conversations. Write them down and study them. Consciously replace the negative ones with positive ones.

The Law of Attraction is constantly bringing to you what you believe and accept. It is a perfect mirror, reflecting back to you your thoughts, feelings, desires, beliefs, and the truth.

My Story

One day I attended a State Fair and there was a man selling umbrellas. He said he could put whatever words we wished on the umbrella. I was selling real estate at that time so I had him put on my umbrella these words. 'Buy Now; He who snoozes loses; the time is right to buy real estate; don't hesitate,' etc.

One day when it was pouring rain I was out showing a client a piece of vacant land. This was about the tenth property I had showed him and I was getting frustrated, not to mention soaking wet, as it was raining and the wind was blowing. He turned to me and said, "Do you think I should buy this property?" I said, "Oh, read my umbrella!" He looked a little shocked and then he began reading. He laughed and said, "You know I like creative people and any realtor who has the guts to put that on their umbrella deserves my sale." So we went back to the office where we dried out a bit and I wrote up the offer which was accepted. So you see the power of words, whether written and/or spoken.

Self-Talk Exercise

Did you know that your subconscious mind is like a bank? It magnifies whatever you deposit into or impress upon it, whether it be wealth or poverty. It never takes a holiday or closes. It is always open. Choose wealth today!

Watch your self-talk. Refrain from saying, "I cannot afford it." When you say this, your subconscious mind (Magic Genie) believes you and carries out your wishes, keeping you broke and creating conditions where you will never be able to afford what you desire. Your subconscious mind says, "He or she says they cannot afford it, so I will have to keep them broke. This is my job to carry out their orders." Rather say, "I choose not to purchase that item at this time," or say, "I choose not to distribute my wealth in this manner." It works wonders.

Self-talk is very important. The way you speak to yourself about yourself determines your life. Past negative thoughts have created your reality today and now you can create a new reality by replacing that negativity with positive, happy self-talk. Your subconscious mind is your humble servant, bringing to you, through the Law of Attraction, exactly what you desire. It believes everything you say. So to recap, if you say, "I am broke," it will keep you broke. Your car gives up the ghost, your washing machine breaks down, or your computer crashes. Your subconscious mind simply does the job of manifesting whatever it is programmed to bring forth. As you change your thoughts and mind, you change your life accordingly.

Thought Watching

For one day write down your thoughts. On a piece of paper or in a small notebook make 3 columns that read:

'Same as yesterday; negative; and positive." Then do some thought-watching. Put a mark under the appropriate column. You will be amazed at what you discover about yourself and your thinking. You have between 50,000 to 60,000 thoughts that run through your mind daily. Where do you think your thoughts are residing?

When I did this exercise I thought I was a very positive person and I was shocked to see how many negative thoughts that I had been harboring during the day. This shows you with great accuracy where your thoughts are residing. If you are not pleased with all these negative thoughts, then you can change them. You created them and you have the power to uncreate them!

Thought Transference

As stated earlier in this book, thought transference is the phenomenon whereby one person tunes into and grasps another's thoughts without any evident, visible means of communication.

You *can* transfer your thoughts to other people. Try it. Find a quiet place, clear your mind, and visualize in complete detail the other person that you wish to have contact you. See what he or she is wearing, their expression, where they are sitting or standing. Are their arms crossed or are they open? Notice every detail about where they are and what is around them.

When you have firmly planted this image in detail in your subconscious mind, then say, "(Name of person), this is (your name). I need to contact you now. Please contact me. Thank you." You can also add love or blessings etc., if you wish. Concentrate and focus on this image and say these words over and over in your mind for about 3-4 minutes. Then go on about your day. You can do this several times daily.

It Worked for Me!

Shortly after I learned this method I gave it a try. I drove past the place of business of the person I wanted to contact me using this method. Would you believe that when I got to my office fifteen minutes after, there was a message from him! When I called him back he said, "I just got the feeling a few minutes ago that I should call you!"

Tiny Speck

Open the flow to your creative channel by visualizing your desire. It is possible to work smarter, not harder, and achieve similar results by using your creative subconscious mind.

Create, think, concentrate and focus on your desires or ideas. Your desire is now a tiny speck in your mind. Increase and magnify it. Make it a small bubble, more bubbles, and then a bigger bubble and see that bubble burst into the beginnings of the desired object of your Affirmation.

For Example

If you are affirming for radiant health, see it first as a small speck of desire deep in your subconscious mind, and then it appears as bubbles containing vivid pictures of you becoming healthier and healthier and then being radiantly healthy. *Visualize* that wonderful picture of you looking and being radiantly healthy, trim and vibrant.

Bring in your 5 physical senses

SEE what you are wearing, Where are you?

HEAR people saying how wonderful you look

FEEL how absolutely healthy and happy you are feeling

SMELL your favourite scent

TASTE a drink of fresh, sparkling water or visualize biting into a juicy apple to complete the five senses

Congratulations - you have just opened and stimulated your creative centre, giving you radiant health. Enjoy!

Go within and ask your higher self to reveal to you when the time is right to take action and what type of action to take.

The 9-Step Creation Process

Step 1 – Clear

Step 2 – Search

Step 3 – Decide

Step 4 – Ask

Step 5 - Creatively Visualize

Step 6 – Accept

Step 7 – Receive

Step 9 – Gratitude

Step 10 - Enjoy Your Creation

Step 1

Clear your mind and take 3 deep breaths. On the OUT breath, breathe out fear, doubt and any form of negativity. On the IN breath, breathe in peace, joy, love and happiness.

Step 2

Search in the files of your mind. Ask yourself, "Is this really my voice and is this really what I want at this time of my life?" After you ask these questions, stop for a moment or two and reflect upon it. Are you ready to have that event, person or material thing in your life? Have you made room for it?

Step 3

Decide. Make a decision and stick with it. When you make a decision and stick with it, you release a great deal of intuitive and powerful energy.

Step 4

Ask with faith believing that your Affirmation manifests as affirmed. Create your Master Affirmation (Your Order to the Universe) saying exactly what you want. Be very specific in your request.

Step 5

Creatively visualize the end result of your Affirmation. Bring in your 5 physical senses--

SEE, HEAR FEEL, SMELL and **TASTE**. Now ACT AS IF you have already received what you are affirming.

Step 6

Accept totally and completely without any limitation or restriction.

Step 7

Receive in joy, anticipation and excitement your completed Affirmation. In other words, TAKE DELIVERY NOW!

Step 8

Say, "Thank you, thank you, thank you," and live in an attitude of gratitude for the blessings you have already received, are receiving and those you are about to receive.

Step 9

Enjoy your Magnificent Creation! Congratulations! You are a powerful Creator!

Sample Master Affirmation for Creation

"I, (your name) use the power of creation wisely. I create positive, happy conditions in my life. I know the power is from within and I use it to the good of all. I am a powerful creation magnet. I am happy, healthy, prosperous and fulfilled to the good of all parties concerned. Thank you, thank you, thank you.

I fully accept"

Signed _____

Dated _____

Affirmations When Properly Done Always Work!

DEATH AFFIRMATION TOOLS

Helping You to Adjust

Closing the Book of Life and Opening the Book of Eternal Life. The Final Destination: The Journey from the Cradle to the Grave

This is the end of the journey. Life's train has taken you from the cradle to the grave. It has been an interesting, intriguing, exciting and, sometimes, a sorrowful and stressful journey.

Everyone who loses a loved one experiences the pain of grief and loss. This is a normal, healthy process that ultimately leads to healing. We each react to a loved one's death in a personal way. The time frame involved is different for every individual. The grieving process could take six to eight months or two, five, 10 years, or more. I once met a widow who was still grieving for her spouse 20 years after his death. Some people never stop grieving. We all grieve in our own ways.

There is a huge difference between grieving and remembering.

My own experience of grief with the death of my two spouses, my mother, father, sister, brother, two business partners, and many friends has taught me that the pain does lessen as time goes by. Time is a great healer.

When you lose that loved one, you lose his or her physical presence, but the relationship still exists. The loved one is still in your heart, mind, and consciousness.

Be Aware of the Stages of Grief

There are several stages of grief involved in handling the death of a loved one.

Shock
- » Initial shock or numbness
- » Tears or emotional release
- » Loneliness
- » In some cases a desire to die

Denial
- » Deep depression
- » Anger, confusion
- » Pain
- » Guilt

Acceptance
- » Hope to go on
- » Struggle to keep on living
- » Plans for the future

Questions to Ask Yourself

Answering the following questions may help you determine what influence your grief has on you.
- » What was your relationship with the deceased? Do you have regrets and unresolved issues?
- » Was the death expected?
- » Was the loved one's illness a long one?
- » Have you had many losses through death recently?
- » Have you resolved grief from past deaths?
- » What is the state of your own mental and emotional health?
- » Do you have other major stress factors in your life?

» Are you dwelling excessively on death and dying?
» Do you suffer from chronic depression, low self-esteem, guilt, or anger?
» Are you holding on to the deceased's clothing and personal effects too long?
» Do you idolize the one who has died, placing him or her on a pedestal?

I found myself idolizing my first husband following his death. When I spoke or thought about him, I only remembered the good times. I blocked out all problems or negativity surrounding our marriage. I was able to correct this when it was pointed out to me by a grief counsellor. Then I began to remember both the good and bad times. This created a healthy, acceptable balance and, as a result, I was able to move on with my life.

Refrain From Making Major Changes

Refrain from making major changes during the first year or two, such as selling your matrimonial home, moving, or changing professions. Become involved with family members or a group of people who can share and understand your loss. Above all--do not feel guilty when you actually begin to feel better.

Tips to Help You Adjust

Give yourself loving kindness
» Be good to yourself
» Eat properly and get plenty of rest and exercise
» Do something you have always wanted to do
» Join a new group of people with similar interests, such as writing, or painting
» If money allows, purchase some new clothes
» Treat yourself to a massage or reflexology treatment

» Plan both long and short trips
» Do not be alarmed if you burst into tears when you hear a favourite song that was special to you and your deceased loved one
» Show your emotions
» Be patient and loving with yourself, as you would be with your child
» Nurture your inner child with gentle loving kindness

Do Not Expect Too Much of Your Children at This Time of Grief

A widowed mother should avoid expecting too much of her children at this time. A young teenage son or daughter should not be given the title and responsibility of being the head of the family. He or she is, and must remain, her child, nothing more.

Be Prepared

Prepare for death while you are here by creating your own belief system about God. When one door closes, another heavenly door opens. Prepare yourself and live every moment to the fullest.

» Be kind to loved ones that you leave grieving your loss
» Have your Last Will and Testament prepared
» Place a list of your assets and liabilities with it
» If you have stock certificates and shares, record them with their respective numbers
» You may also wish to list what personal items you would like to distribute and to name the recipients
» List the bank or banks that you do business with, as well as your accounts and account numbers
» Keep your personal papers in one place

Never spend your precious time complaining or dwelling on your illnesses, hurts, or worries. Experience peace by doing your Affirmation Program faithfully. Give thanks every day to God for a glorious, new day.

Sample Master Affirmation for Being at Peace

"I, (your name), deserve to be able to release and now do release my fear and doubt. I am at peace. I know this is the last period of my life here on earth. I am ready to complete my final journey. When it is time to cross over, I know the s will be with me. Any fear of dying leaves my body now. I am safe. I ask the Angel of Death to be with me to help me make my transition smooth and peaceful. I am happy, secure, and peaceful. I know that dying is a part of life and I accept that fact and am at peace. I leave a legacy of love and loving kindness for my loved ones and all humanity. I release myself to my Heavenly Father with peace, to the good of all parties concerned. Thank you, thank you, thank you.

I fully accept"

Signed _____

Dated _____

Address _____

Affirmations When Properly Done Always Work!

FAITH AFFIRMATION TOOLS

Mustard Seed

It is always a good idea to apply faith when doing your Affirmations. It says in the Bible, "If ye have faith as a grain of mustard seed ye shall say unto this mountain remove hence to yonder place and it shall remove and nothing shall be impossible unto you."

I affix (put a piece of clear scotch tape over the tiny seed) a mustard seed on the right hand corner of all my Master Affirmations. When I see the tiny seed it reminds me of just how little faith we need to create our desires.

Fulfilled Affirmation Book

When my Affirmations manifest, I put a *big* check mark on the Master Affirmation with a felt pen, together with the date it actually happened.

I place it in my *Fulfilled Affirmation Book*. To expand and increase my faith when I begin a new Affirmation, all I have to do is look back at all the Affirmations that have successfully manifested.

It brings them to my attention and consciousness and also increases my faith. I have many huge, loose-leaf books marked *Fulfilled Affirmations,* from all phases of my life. The good news is that *you* can have the same results.

Sample Master Affirmation

"My faith increases daily. I believe in myself and my life. I ask and I receive and accept in an attitude of gratitude. I am very thankful for all the blessings I have received, are receiving and for those I am about to receive. I am a powerful creator to the good of all parties concerned. Thank you, thank you, thank you.

I fully accept"

Signed _____

Dated _____

Address _____

Affirmations When Properly Done Always Work!

FEAR AFFIRMATION TOOLS

F – False
E - Evidence
A - Appearing
R - Real
My version: **F**ind **E**nlightening **A**nswers **R**eadily Fear Dragon

Fear can be a block that keeps you from doing something you wish to do. For example, a fear of flying could prevent you from experiencing many wonderful travelling experiences.

Imagine your fear in front of you; see it in the form of a fear dragon.

> » How big is it?
> » What color is it?
> » What shape is it?
> » How close is it?
> » Can you feel its breath?
> » How hot is it?
> » Do you feel uncomfortable?

Now mentally take a club and place it in one of your hands and push the fear dragon away from you. You do not wish to burn yourself. You are stronger than any fear dragon.

Ask it to speak to you. Say, "Have you anything to say to me?" Listen with your inner ear. Now be firm with the fear dragon. Inform it that it has no place in your body or around you and that it has to go.

If the fear dragon tries to hang around, say again, "You must go. You are not welcome in or around my being." Say, "Fear dragon, you have no power over me. You are helpless. I am the powerful force here and you must obey me. I am the boss." Be firm and the fear dragon will vanish completely. Now, in its place, create an image of what you wish to accomplish.

For example, see yourself on an airplane embarking on some exciting adventure. See yourself surrounded by a pink, soft bubble — being safe and content, enjoying the flight to wherever you desire. This technique is very effective in banishing any limiting fears, and helping you achieve what you want.

Fear Zoo

You might wish to put your fears into proper perspective by forming your own *fear zoo* – a place where you can put all your fears. You may fear a wild tiger in the jungle but would you fear a tiger in a cage in a zoo? My own *fear zoo* is where I place all my fears.

I visualize my fear of closed-in spaces as a ferocious tiger, my fear of rejection as an angry gorilla, and my fear of dying as a giant giraffe. I visualize my fear of poverty and lack as two grizzly bears and any other smaller fears as cantankerous, quarrelsome monkeys. I visit them as often as possible. I look forward to our conversations and discussions! I consider them great, valuable teachers and learn from my experiences with them. At times, I just sit quietly among them, feeling their presence and allowing them to feel and experience my presence. When you give fear a name and form and speak directly to it, its hold over you is lessened and its power is scattered. What is your greatest fear? Name it, give it form, and speak directly to it in a controlled, safe atmosphere.

What animals will you choose? Your fear becomes manageable when you do this exercise. As long as you continue to grow and learn, fear will be your constant companion. Isn't it better to manage and control fear than to let it control you? When I taught the Fear Zoo Exercise to a 3rd grade class, one student visualized her fear of heights as a huge giraffe. After doing this exercise, she discovered to her absolute delight that her intense fear of heights had completely vanished.

Sample Master Affirmation for Releasing Fear

"I, (your name), deserve to be and now am happy. My life is full, rich, and rewarding. I live in the now. Any and all negative, unwanted fear leaves my body and I am 100 % healthy. I enjoy being calm, peaceful, and phobia-free. I thank God daily for all my blessings and fully accept them. I am completely free of fear and safe. I am happy, to the good of all parties concerned. Thank you, thank you, thank you.

I fully accept"

Signed _____

Dated _____

Address _____

Affirmations When Properly Done Always Work!

FORGIVENESS & RELEASING AFFIRMATION TOOLS

Affirmations of Denial

An Affirmation of Denial is a declaration of rejection, as compared to a positive Affirmation which is a declaration of acceptance. They are used to free one's self of lack, limitations, false beliefs, and erroneous concepts.

Affirmations of Denial are powerful toxin cleansers and releasers. They are helpful in assisting us to uncover and unravel hidden blockages. Be prepared for some surprising, unexpected, sometimes negative thoughts, feelings, and memories from the past to surface when doing Affirmations of Denial. This process may uncover previous negative programming and work to diffuse it.

As in the following example, when you examine your denial statements you can readily see where your blockages are, and then you can go about releasing them. Tell negativity it has to go immediately. Speak with authority. Affirmations of Denial will also show you with great certainty how deeply you desire your Master Affirmation. Do the following exercise to discover where you have blockages.

Uncovering and Discovering Exercise

Beside each of your Affirmations, write down any mental objections that come to mind. Let's look at an example that is very common. Every one of us has, at one time or another, experienced blockages that keep us from loving self and others. Some of these blockages can actually prevent you from attaining your heart's desires.

My Affirmation　　　**The Blockage**

I am lovable	*No one likes me*
I am a smart person	*Co-workers think I am slow*
I am respected	*Everyone looks down on me.*

In this manner, you are recognizing your negative feelings by writing them on a piece of paper. Examine each one of these statements, then take a deep breath and release them. Ask yourself how long you have held these thoughts and beliefs and you will see how deeply they are ingrained. Where did they come from? Do you still want them to be part of your being? Are they serving you to your highest good? If the answer is "No," release them today.

Continue this exercise until there is no negativity left. Record and release all negativity in the right column and let it go completely. Use the forgiveness and releasing tools in the next section to help you. You will be happy to note that soon your right column will become more positive and will start to agree with your Affirmations.

Now it could look like this:

My Affirmation	**The Truth**
I am lovable	*People are paying more attention to me*
I am a smart person	*People ask me for advice and my opinions*
I am respected	*People respect me and my opinions*

Here's another example:

My Affirmation	The Blockage
Money is good	*No, I hate it*
Money is good	*It creates all kinds of problems*
Money is good.	*I think it is dirty*

Once you have recorded and released all negativity in the right column, letting it go completely, it could start to look like this:

My Affirmation	The Truth
Money is good	*It did help me get my teeth fixed*
Money is good	*It bought food for that poor family*
Money is good	*I now see how money really is good*

With a bit of work, you can transform your beliefs and clear the way for your Affirmations to manifest. Now you will be able to focus on what you want, not what you do not want.

Letter from Self to Self

This is a letter is a letter that you write from your Higher Self to another's Higher Self, sometimes referred to as 'An Angel Letter.' When writing from your to another's, you are communicating on spiritual or higher level, filled with loving kindness, peace, joy, and happiness.

I have used this Angel Letter Method on numerous occasions. The quickest results have occurred when this letter is written a total of fifteen times. I have tried it with 7, 10, 21 and 30 and always the times I do it 15 works the best for me. Read what the mystics have to say about it further down.

Letter Success

One of my readers, Beth had a bear problem. There was this bear that thought he was her pet. He hung around her house and even would lie on her front steps as if he was a family pet. She was exasperated and had done everything she could when she spoke to me about it. She told me she was planning on putting poison in some raw meat and putting it in one of her trees and that way the bear would eat it and die. I said, "Oh Beth, please, please don't do that!" Let's do the letter first. She reluctantly agreed and we created the following letter.

Letter Procedure

To the Angel of the Bear that hangs out in my yard.

"I send you God's love; I bless you and I thank you for not coming into my yard again and for finding a place in your natural habitant where you will be happy. Please know you are not welcome here. Love from the Angel of Beth." She put her street address. She dated and signed it. She kept this copy in her wallet (purse) and then she scribbled the same verbiage out 14 more times, to make a total of 15.

Well the bear got the message loud and clear and never came back into her yard, but Beth found out that he went a couple of blocks away into a neighbour's yard. She asked me if she should knock on the door and tell them about the letter. I told her that would be totally up to her. Then Beth said, "But why didn't the Affirmation work? Why didn't the bear find a place in the bush to live?" I replied, "But Beth it did work! The bear is gone from your place and look around you, this WAS his natural habitant until man started building homes on this ravine."

Such is the power of the letter.

Another Letter Success

A Reader writes . . .

"My daughter Wendy and her husband Jeff just moved into a new apartment. The neighbour next door was playing her music very loud and until 2:00 a.m. and later, and they could not sleep. The music equipment was against the wall where their bedroom was located."

When she called me asking what she could do, of course, I recommended that she contact a person of the Strata Council and write a formal complaint. This is a new building and they were just in the process of forming a Strata Council and the woman who was temporarily in charge was on holidays for six weeks. So I suggested to a that she suggest that Wendy write an Letter to the person or persons living next to her apartment who were playing the loud music all hours of the night, which she did!

"To the Angel of the Person(s) Next door to my Apartment at _____ (she put her address),

I send you God's love; I bless you and I thank you for not playing your music so loud and so late and for being considerate of us, as we are considerate of you. We are all harmonious to the good of all parties concerned. Thank you, thank you, thank you.

Love from the Angel of your neighbour (her name)."

She did as I suggested and wrote the first copy very legibly on a recipe card and placed it in her wallet and took it out and read it over many times during the day.

She also scribbled out the other 14 copies and destroyed them. So, in actuality, she wrote 15 copies of the letter.

She reported that the young girl who was living next door moved out and her parent moved back in. She ran into him in the elevator and told him about it. He apologized and promised that would never happen again and said he would move his musical equipment on the other side of the room so it would not be right against this bedroom wall.

She was so excited and happy and now is enjoying peace and quiet and, most of all, a good night's sleep in her apartment thank to the Letter Process. I have many, many other stories about the success of the letters.

Note:

This letter is NEVER given or mailed to anyone. It is kept in your possession so you can read it over whenever you wish. This is not meant to hurt or upset anyone. This method can be used for many situations such as communicating with a lover, spouse, family member, friend, co-worker, employer, bank manager, noisy neighbor, or any person, and even with a mouse, bear, ant, antlers (inanimate objects), and more.

You could even write an Angel Letter to a prospective employer. Write, "To the Angel of the Decision-Maker or Manager: I send you divine wisdom and I thank you for considering my application and for hiring me, to the good of all parties concerned. Thank you from the Angel of your prospective employee."

The person who's Angel you are writing to never sees the letter.

Write the full letter out 15 times, because this is the number mystics believe has the power to destroy negative thoughts. If you wish to change your Angel Letter, you could write out the new one and staple it to the original. On the new one, in red ink, write: 'Revised Edition.'

When I do this exercise, I write a master copy of the Letter out on a 3." x 5." card and keep it in my wallet. I read over the other 14 letters, and then I burn them. (I have done this process of writing the letter only three, 10, and 12 times, but the process works best doing it 15 times).

You only need to do the Angel Letter procedure once (for each situation that is). This is a simple, powerful exercise that produces unbelievable, positive results. Do it and see for yourself.

Sample Angel Letter

"To the Angel of _____:

I love you (or I send you God's love), I bless you, and I thank you for _____

_____

_____

_____

_____(State what you wish to ask the Angel to do.)_____

_____

To the good of all parties concerned. Thank you, thank you, thank you.

Love from the Angel of _____.

Signed _____

Date: _____

Letter to Your Own Angel

The following letter may be addressed to your personal Angel, affirming the assistance and support you may draw upon from the Divine Realms.

To My Personal Angel:

"I love you; I bless you and thank you for assisting in creating harmonious working conditions for me. Also, thank you for my employer recognizing my good work and rewarding me accordingly. I enjoy regular raises and bonuses. I am happy and fulfilled to the good of all parties concerned. Thank you, thank you, thank you. I am healthy and happy, to the good of all parties concerned. Thank you, thank you, thank you. Love from (your name)."

Signed_____

Date _____

Address _____

_____

Balloon Releasing

When you desire to forgive and release negative beliefs, memories and thoughts about any negative situation or about not having money and being poor do the following exercise.

Visualize all those negative thoughts, beliefs and memories being placed into a hot air balloon securely attached to the ground by two ropes. See yourself standing close to the balloon. As you cut the ropes attached to the balloon, say:

"I, (your name), now release all negative thoughts and beliefs about being rich. I now release them with unconditional love. I let them go in peace with loving kindness and detachment from the outcome. I am happy to the good of all parties concerned. Thank you, thank you, thank you."

It is important to engage the 5 physical senses.

SEE	the balloon floating up into the sky
HEAR	the ropes making a snapping sound as the balloon tugs against them
FEEL	the scissors between your fingers
SMELL	the odor of the ropes
TASTE	the brisk, fresh, clean air or bite into a juicy apple

Note:

Because of the environmental hazard to wildlife and marine life, we suggest you do the above exercise in your mind, rather than release a real balloon into the air.

Blackboard & Eraser

Visualize in your mind's eye a huge blackboard. Now take a piece of chalk and write down all the people and things that you need to forgive in your life, perhaps people who have hurt you. Beside each name, write what that person did to you. Look at the blackboard and read your words, feeling the hurt.

Take a deep breath and let it go completely. Allow and watch each one of them dissolve. Pick up an eraser and rub out everything you have just written. Feel that you are completely forgiving and releasing that person to his or her highest good, with loving kindness. A h h, feel how absolutely free and wonderful you feel.

I use an emerald-green eraser brush because green represents change and growth, but you may use pink or any color that appeals to you.

Blanket Exercise

Some people like this exercise because it brings them back to their childhood or many years ago. They learn how people in those days handled their anger and it gives them confidence that they can do the same. Others may prefer to release their anger "beating up a sheet." instead of themselves.

Pretend you are back in the olden days. In your mind, place a blanket on a clothesline. Take a huge stick, baseball bat, broom or whatever you wish and keep on hitting the blanket over and over with all the energy you can muster up. (They used to beat the sheets in those days to get rid of the dust, dirt and grim.) You are beating your imaginary sheet getting rid of your anger, frustration, negativity and feelings of not deserving to be prosperous, always have to struggle, thinking there is not enough to go around, that you will never be wealthy, etc. Keep on until you are exhausted.

Car Exercise

One of the quickest and easiest ways of getting rid of negative feelings and memories is to shout out your anger or just get into your car, roll up the windows, and drive.

Get into your car and drive out in the country (or roll up your car windows). Find a place where you can safely park and start yelling and screaming at the top of your lungs all you want. Call yourself every name under the sun; be angry at yourself for putting yourself in this state of poverty and lack *(just for a short period of time)*. When your energy is all used up, stop for several moments, relax, and give thanks for the completed release.

Cleansing Body Exercise

Whenever you feel that your body needs a 'house cleaning,' you may wish to do the Cleansing the Body. This is a great 'pick-me- up when you are feeling a little down or out of sorts.

Exercise
» Sit quietly
» Visualize that a soothing mist in your favourite color is gently calming your thoughts and clearing your mind
» Take several deep breaths, then exhale any negative, unwanted feelings and thoughts.
» Breathe in positive, happy feelings and thoughts
» Visualize that you have an opening in the top of your head — like a teapot does

See your favourite color pouring into your body in the consistency of honey. Let the beautiful substance flow throughout your body, down into your arms, your fingers, torso, legs, toes . . . every part of you.

Now completely release all negativity from every part of your body. Fill yourself with peace, joy, love, and happiness. You feel refreshed, invigorated, and rejuvenated.

End the exercise by saying, "Thank you, thank you, thank you."

Cup Emptying Forgiveness Exercise

If you feel you have any negativity about anyone or anything, now is the time to deal with it and release it.

Also release any feelings of low self-esteem, not deserving, etc.

For optimum results, perform this exercise every morning and evening.

Use a cup or mug. Take a pen and masking tape and print the words, 'All my negativity and doubt,' then put the label on the cup. Sit with the cup in your hands and visualize all unhappy feelings surrounding your negative beliefs dripping into the water from your eyes, ears, nose, and mouth.

When you feel that process is complete, take the cup to the sink and pour out that water, saying the following Affirmation.

"All negative feelings now pour out of my heart, life, and being. As I pour this water down the sink, with my negative feelings in it, I know I can never get it back. I am happy, healthy, safe, and protected to the good of all parties concerned. Thank you, thank you, thank you."

When the cup or mug is empty, just say, "Healed consciousness."

Fiery Anger Release Exercise

Very Important! Only do this exercise in your mind!

Whenever you are experiencing extreme anger, you are affecting your whole body. When you put a 'd' in front of anger it becomes *danger*. Release negative anger before it has as chance to negatively affect your body, life, and emotions.

In your mind's eye see yourself standing on a white, sandy beach. You see some twigs, sticks, and pieces of dry wood lying around. Feel yourself picking them up and making a huge pile in the middle of the deserted beach.

There are no trees, buildings, or people nearby. Just wide open space.

Now face the pile of sticks and wood and see the fiery anger of being in this state of lack, of never having enough money, of always having to scrimp, and the feeling that life is not worth living, coming out of you. Feel these feelings and statements rising from the tips of your toes. As you breathe it out, this inner fire ignites the huge pile of sticks and it catches on fire. When all the fiery anger has left your body, bring in your 5 physical senses.

SEE the huge flames of the fire, standing backing at a safe distance

HEAR the crackling sound

SMELL the smoke

FEEL the heat against your body

TASTE a drink of water

Watch it as it burns every stick and piece of wood right down to the sandy beach (this could take a few minutes or longer). Wait for it as long as it takes.

When the fire has burned down and becomes ashes on the beach, watch as a huge wave washes over the ashes and all the fire is put out. Savor that feeling of releasing all your anger and clearing the way for great wealth that is coming. You are feeling so much better and possibly a little drained, so take a short rest.

You may need to repeat this exercise whenever you feel anger welling up in you.

Letter to Self Exercise

Write yourself a letter of appreciation and encouragement, saying how much you appreciate, respect and love yourself.

After I have successfully handled a difficult, delicate situation, I find it very therapeutic to write a letter of self-praise and appreciation and mail it to myself. It is such a treat to receive the letter in the mail, open it up, and read it. I mailed one such letter from Washington State and it was lost in the mail. It was finally delivered several months later. I had completely forgotten about it. When I received and opened it, I was stunned and totally unprepared for what feelings it brought up in me. It certainly had a huge impact on me! Try it and see what effect it has on you.

Remember to give yourself honest appreciation for a job well done. Be lavish with your praise. When you praise, you actually **p** raise.

Letter to Your Parent(s) Exercise

You may wish to try this simple letter writing exercise which encourages releasing old memories and getting on with your life.

I recommend that you deal with only one person (parent), circumstance, or situation at a time. Write the letter, remembering all hurts, anger, resentments, and injustices. Like how you never had new clothes and had to wear hand-me-downs, never had the things other children had and could not afford to attend university.

As you put these words on paper, they are removed and released from your being.

See, hear, feel, smell, and taste your anger, frustration and hurt. Read the letter and feel the pain. Read the letter, feel the pain and then release it together with any and all negativity surrounding that event of being poor, people teasing you or any negative circumstance. Burn or destroy the letter immediately. Burning reduces the anger and negativity to ashes.

You could also shred it or cut it up into tiny pieces and flush it down the toilet. Never leave it lying around as someone could read it and become hurt. It is not the object here to hurt anyone. It is sufficient that you have operated and taken the hurt and negativity (emotional cancer) out of your body by the simple method of the written word. This process works even if the person with whom you are angry is deceased.

Pillow Punching Exercise

The Pillow Exercise is a very simple, yet effective method of releasing negativity. Get a pillow and pound it over and over. Say whatever comes to mind. Get the anger and rage out of being poor, in a state of lack, and of never having enough money. Pound it over and over until you become exhausted. Then stop, take a rest and say, "Thank you, thank you, thank you for my wonderful prosperity and perfect peace."

Toothbrush (Extended Toothbrush Forgiveness Exercise)

When you get up in the morning and just after you brush your teeth, look at yourself in the mirror and say, "Hey self, you are a mighty fine person. I now forgive everyone and everything that has ever hurt me. I now forgive myself. I love, respect and approve of myself just the way I am." This includes forgiving any person, circumstance or situation that you feel is unfair to you or that has hurt you. Things you thought you had forgotten years ago will come into your memory.

When you say *ever*, you go back to creation and right back to when you were in your mother's womb. If too many memories surface at the same time, just say, "One at a time please." Then deal with each negative memory, briefly feeling the pain, then releasing it and letting it go completely.

Sample Master Affirmation to Overcome & Release Fear

"I, (your name), deserve to be and now am happy. My life is full, rich, and rewarding. I live in the now. Any and all negative, unwanted fear leaves my body and I am 100% healthy. I enjoy being calm, peaceful, and phobia-free. I thank God daily for all my blessings and fully accept them. I am completely free of negative fear and safe. I am happy, to the good of all parties concerned. Thank you, thank you, thank you.

I fully accept"

Signed _____

Dated _____

Address _____

Affirmations When Properly Done Always Work!

GENERAL AFFIRMATION TOOLS

21 Day Agreement

When making agreements, Affirmations, listening to tapes, etc. we always encourage you to do it for a minimum of 21 days as studies have shown that it takes 21 days to make a habit.

Asking Your Subconscious Mind for Answers

When you require an answer to a question, think of the issue involved and request the perfect solution just before dropping off to sleep. Then say to your subconscious mind, "Please answer," and wait for the answer to appear.

Attitude of Gratitude Exercise

When you get up in the morning say, "Thank you, thank you, thank you for another day." Be grateful for all your blessings. When you go to bed at night just before dropping off to sleep, start counting your blessings, naming them one by one and give thanks. You will find more and more blessings to be thankful for as the Law of Attraction kicks in. Live in an attitude of gratitude. Saying thank you in advance is a powerful tool.

I believe when we say "thank you, thank you, thank you" in advance, we obligate the planet for more good or we open the flood gates of heaven for even more blessings.

Cancel, Cancel, or Delete, Delete Exercise

This tool is about breaking negative cycles by changing our way of thinking, talking, and listening.

We can say, "Cancel, cancel" or "Delete, delete" to negative conversations, words, thoughts, and actions from self and others. For example, if someone says hurtful things to you, simply say to yourself, "Cancel, cancel, I am happy." In this way, those hurtful statements will not be able to enter into your consciousness (your inner computer) and you will not have to deal with them. You could even stamp your foot as you say, "Cancel, cancel, that's not true," to any negative words from others (or from your own mind). It is very important to immediately add a positive statement to fill the space you have just created by saying, "Cancel, cancel" since nature abhors a vacuum and will rush to fill it--and you wouldn't want it to be filled with more negativity!

Car Exercise

One of the quickest and easiest ways of getting rid of negative feelings and memories is to shout out your anger or just get into your car, roll up the windows, and drive.

Get into your car and drive out in the country (or roll up your car windows). Find a place where you can safely park, and start yelling and screaming at the top of your lungs all you want. Call yourself every name under the sun; tell yourself that you are upset because you put yourself into this state of poverty and lack *(just for a short period of time)*. When your energy is all used up, stop for several moments, relax, and give thanks for the completed release.

Clear Front & Back Exercise—Eliminating Traffic Jams

When I am in a traffic jam or attempting to catch a plane or ferry, I simply say, with great feeling, "Clear front and back." If I am turning onto a busy street, I say, "Clear side to side." I always add, "To the good of all parties concerned." This exercise has helped me avoid frustration, keep appointments, cross borders, and catch trains, airplanes, and ferries on time.

You can transfer your thought forms from one driver of a vehicle to another. I applied this principle very successfully during a trip with two friends. While driving to the ferry, in heavy traffic, we all concentrated and said with great feeling and expectancy, "Clear front and back." The cars around us just seemed to vanish into thin air. One truck actually pulled over to let us go by. As a result, we arrived at the ferry on time.

Clear, Search and Retrieve Exercise

When you need to remember an incident or a person's name, close your eyes gently and say to yourself, "Clear, search, and retrieve." Clear your mind of all thoughts. Now go into the files of your mind and select the one that contains the answer to your question. Visualize retrieving that file that contains the answer to your question. Say "Thank you, thank you, thank you for the correct answer."

I use this Affirmation Tool almost daily. One lady emailed me that she had failed her exam because she froze up when she starting answering the question. She said that she was going to re-write it and how could she pass and did I have any Affirmation Tools to help her? I shared this tool with her and her second email said, "Wow, did that Affirmation tool ever work--I passed with 89%. When I went in to write my exam I felt confident because I knew I had studied and knew my material and I knew I also had the Clear, Search and Retrieve tool to help me. I believed in it and I used it with great success. I cannot thank you enough!"

Empathy Shoes Exercise

Even though I like to use this exercise with children, I find it interesting to do myself.

In my mind, when I was upset with another person, I put on a pair of their shoes. I make them look funny so it makes me laugh. Then, in my mind, I picture this person very vividly and then I walk around in his or her shoes for an hour or more. During this time, I think how they must feel about the situation without letting my own feelings cloud the picture. When I feel I have completed the exercise, I file it in my mind for future reference and I go about my day. This really does help me see that person and/or situation in a different, new, and more positive light.

Energy Intact Exercise

When you simply have to be in the company of a negative person or persons, sit with your ankles crossed and put your hands together. This way you are not allowing any negativity from the other person to enter your body. You stop any drain on your energy and keep your own positive energy intact.

Glass of Water Exercise

Take a glass of water, hold it in your hand, and visualize the question within the water. Drink one-half of the glass of water before going to bed, asking your subconscious mind for the answer by repeating the words, "Please answer." Ask for any relevant information, already stored in your memory bank, to be revealed to you. Ponder your problem before you fall asleep, examining it from all angles and instructing your subconscious mind to come up with the perfect answer. It will automatically provide the solution. Drink the rest of the water upon rising. Usually, the answer will flash into your mind in the morning or later that day. It can present itself as an event, thought, idea, experience, hunch, and words from another person, something you read, a feeling, or a knowingness.

Be certain to say "Thank you" three times, in anticipation of what you will be receiving from the Universe. By emphasizing your gratitude in advance, you are telling the Universe you fully expect your Affirmation to manifest. This expectancy further empowers and reinforces your Affirmation.

Hourglass Exercise

When I am overwhelmed, thinking "How can I ever get everything done that I need to do today?" I do the Hourglass Exercise. I have an hourglass on my desk close to my computer. I watch each grain of sand going through the tiny neck of the hourglass and think about how just one grain of sand is able to get through at a time.

If I try to force more than one grain, it clogs up and stops. I use this in my life, doing only one task at one time, and that way everything gets done.

Swallowing a Whole Apple Exercise

If you swallowed a large apple whole, you would choke. If you cut the apple up into bite-size pieces and ate one at a time, you would accomplish the task of eating the apple. A baby first crawls, walks, then runs. It is so important to do the first step, which is deciding what you really desire, then to do the appropriate Affirmation that produces the desired result. Don't try to tackle the whole job at once!

Take Your Life Off Lay-Away Exercise

Sit down and really think about your life. Make a list of the things you are waiting to do someday off into the future. Also add things that you feel you cannot do right now because of this or that and things you are holding off doing. Then say, "Right here and right now I take my life off lay-away and start living in the present, this present moment."

Then enjoy all those things you only thought about.

Light house Exercise

Have you ever been in a lighthouse? When I visited one I was amazed at how many magnifications that light went through to make it brilliant, bright, and clear, and to shine out into the water to help guide captains and people safely to shore. I thought to myself that no matter how strong the storm was, how high the waves, how much lightning and thunder was going on around that beam of light, nothing could touch it as it kept on doing its job shining brightly--a port in the time of storm. If I was connected to God's wonderful power and light like that beam, it would not matter what was going on around me--I would be bright, clear and steadfast.

Magic Magnetic Circle Exercise

When you get up in the morning, clear your mind of any negative thoughts. Forgive everyone and everything that has ever hurt you.

Say, "I, (your name), now love, respect and approve of myself, just the way I am." Stand facing the window, slowly turning from left to right (clockwise) with your arms outstretched, saying the following Affirmation:

Magic Magnetic Circle Master Affirmation

Short-Form Affirmation: Full of powerful, positive magnetism.

Be certain and bring in the five physical senses when doing this exercise.

SEE	your arms outstretched from your sides
HEAR	the sound of your voice saying the Affirmation
SMELL	your favorite scent or flower
FEEL	yourself as you turn slowly around clockwise
TASTE	a juicy apple or a drink of fresh, sparkling water

No, it is not selfish to magnetize these wonderful things to yourself first, since you cannot give to others without first giving to yourself. You cannot give from an empty cup. You need to love and respect yourself before you can expect others to do so.

Magnifying Glass Exercise

Write out all your blessings and then place a magnifying glass over the words and ask them to multiply.

I decided to do this experiment. I took a strong magnifying glass and a piece of newspaper outside on a bright and sunny day. The sun's rays were very strong. I held the magnifying glass steady over the newspaper for a short period of time and it caught fire.

Then I decided to keep everything the same; that is, the same magnifying glass, same type of newspaper, same distance, same time of day and I only changed ONE thing. Instead of holding the magnifying glass steadily over the newspaper I moved it from side to side and nothing happened. It did not catch on fire!

Why not? Because I was scattering the focus. So I likened that to doing my Master Affirmation where I concentrated on what was written and did not let my thoughts and mind wander from one thing to another. I kept them focused on the manifestation of that particular Affirmation. The results were absolutely fantastic!

This is the power of focus. I never forgot the simple and powerful lesson that this magnifying glass and sun's rays taught me.

One Step at a Time Exercise

Every journey begins with the first step—one step at a time, one miracle at a time. Be aware that every goal or Affirmation consists of several steps, each one based on the previous one. The first step of any journey or program is of prime importance. Once the steps are clearly formed in your mind like a picture, they are easy to follow.

These steps are the Master Plan (The Affirmation Program) that carries you to the materialization of your goals and Affirmations.

One of my students told me that her Affirmations were coming true in stages or baby-steps. I advised her to put Step One, Step Two, and Step Three on her Master Affirmations and check off each step as it manifested for her. This is a faith-builder.

Everything in life is like a progression of steps. Tackle one task at a time, one step at a time and one grain of sand at a time.

Once you have done your Master Affirmation, analyze it and break it down into steps. Number the steps in a way that is logical to you. If necessary, break it down into even smaller steps. Check out each part. Is it reasonable? Will it work? Be flexible. Change and revise your Affirmations as often as necessary. As you change, your Affirmations change. Make adjustments and allow room for the unexpected. Welcome new ideas and be self-disciplined and persistent. Perseverance means hanging in there when all the odds appear to be stacked against you.

Cut Your Apple into Pieces Exercise

If you were to try and swallow a whole apple at a time, you could not or you would choke. When you cut the apple into bite size pieces you can accomplish eating the whole apple, one piece at a time.

Pail of Water Analogy Exercise

This demonstrates how to get rid of negative emotions!

When you are feeling a bit down and/or your conscious-ness, thoughts and mind are negative or becoming nega-tive, you may wish to do the following simple exercise. It shows you, with great certainty, that you can change those negative thoughts and emotions to uplifting and positive ones by continually being aware of what you are thinking and, should they be negative, then start bombarding them with wonderful, uplifting, positive, happy thoughts.

Over time, you will see that your attitude and whole energy field changes for the better. Just like cleaning the pail of water, you have cleansed your mind, consciousness and emotions. I use this method many times, with great, sometimes unbelievable results when I start to feel nega-tive. Many of my readers have reported great success with the method as well.

Take a pail of water and fill it with dirty water. Place it in the sink and open the tap so a very small amount of clear, clean water flows into the pail. Watch how eventu-ally all the dirty water overflows and in its place is the clean, clear water.

This is a great exercise to do when you feel that your mind needs some mental house cleaning. You will be amazed to see that dirty water become clear and clean.

Parking Spaces Exercise

Do you ever experience difficulty locating a parking space and find yourself driving around and around in frustration? By using the Affirmation Process regularly, you can mentally affirm to yourself that you have the perfect parking space in front of the place you are about to visit - that the perfect parking spot will become avail-able to you exactly where you want it. Whenever I do that, someone usually vacates a space just as I arrive and I drive right into it.

Photograph Exercise

When you are experiencing difficulty saying what you want to another person, do this exercise. Before you do this exercise, make sure you have done your forgiveness and releasing exercises and are ready to manifest as affirmed.

Place a photograph of him or her in their favorite chair. Now start a conversation looking at the photograph, just as if you were actually speaking to that person. Talk about the issue that is bothering you. Say what you think and tell him or her what you are willing to do to correct it and ask for their help. Ask that person to really listen to you and hear what you are saying. This Affirmation Tool works so well because your subconscious mind will remember that you have already said these words when you speak in person. Also, it helps you keep your emotions balanced.

Testimonial for Roy

When I got married the second time, I was experiencing difficulty saying what I really wanted to say to my husband, Roy. So I took a large, colored picture of him and placed it in his chair while he was at work. I started a dialogue with the picture. I said, "Hey Roy, listen up. I need to talk to you about . . . . " (here I added what I felt the issue was). As I was in the middle of my conversation with Roy's picture, the mailman came to the door.

Since it was summer, I had the door open. He was a friend of ours and he looked around and said, "I didn't think Roy was home. I don't see his truck." I said, "No, he is not home, and I am talking to his picture." He sort of smiled as he was rather used to some of my 'far out' ways, and asked me about the process.

He also asked me if I thought it would work with his wife, Wendy. I said, "What do you have to lose trying it?" Several weeks later he reported that he used the process speaking to Wendy about her spending habits. Then later he was able to sit down and calmly discuss the matter without bringing up anger in her. He loved the exercise and said it sure helped his marriage, and said he is now telling people to try it.

Picture Power Exercise

I once read about a soldier in a prison camp who practiced his golf game daily in his mind. He visualized it so many times that it became a natural part of him. When he was released and physically played golf, his performance was outstanding. His mind could not tell the difference between the game he visualized in his mind and the one he actually played on the golf course.

Effective coaches also teach team members the art of creative visualization, but this process is not restricted to athletes. People from all walks of life use it every day with fantastic results. Creative visualization empowers and directs your mind to work *for* you, rather than *against* you.

Quicksand Vision

Are you an empathic helper or an enabler? Today we hear a great deal about enablers — people that help others stay in their negative situations.

I feel there is a fine line between helping another person and jumping into their challenge and going down with them.

1st *Frame*

I distinctly saw, in my mind's eye, a person (I do not know whether it was a man or woman). This person looked like they were sinking quickly. He or she was in a state of panic and yelled loudly, "Help me Dr. Evers."

Next Frame

I saw a picture of me jumping in with him or her.

Next Frame

I jumped in and I felt as if I was drowning in the quicksand with that person.

Next Frame

There was absolute total darkness. This frightened me for a moment or two and then the vision continued.

Next Frame

The same picture of a person in quick sand yelling for help re-appeared.

Next Frame

This frame showed a picture of me standing on the ground. I took a strong rope and tied a Girl Guide knot around a sturdy tree.

Next Frame

I tossed that person the end of the rope.

Next Frame

A picture of that person taking hold of the end of the rope and quickly and safely pulling themselves out of the quicksand unto the shore (ground).

Final Frame

I was hugging the person and we were both very happy.

Important Lesson for Me

It is important to always be there to help people with their life lessons but not to write the lessons for them. And I asked myself, "Who appointed me to write others' earthly exams?" The challenges and situations they are experiencing are for their own growth and we, as teachers, are here to help them along the way. Also, it showed me with great clarity that it is so important to share these wonderful Affirmation Tools with others so they can help themselves.

Remember in the Bible it says that God helps them that help themselves.

Random Acts of Kindness Exercise

Do at least one random act of kindness every day.

I believe we should all be doing Random Acts of Kindness every single day. There is always an opportunity to be kind, say something kind or do something kind to another person.

On my radio show, The **Dr. Anne Marie Evers Show,** every Saturday I devote 15 minutes to speaking about and reporting random acts of kindness. Pay it forward. It is amazing to watch a random act of kindness and see the joy it brings to the person receiving the kindness, the person doing the act and the people watching.

Ripple Effect Exercise

What we think and do and say ripples out into the world. If you take a bowl of water and drop a small pebble into it, you can watch how the ripples go out from the area where the pebble was dropped. I like to do this with children so they can see this tangibly. Your words are like that pebble when dropped in, causing a ripple effect in your world.

Sandwich Exercise

When it is absolutely necessary to give constructive criticism, sandwich it with praise. For example, if your daughter has a very messy room, you might say--

1. "Holly, you are such a wonderful daughter." (one slice of bread)
2. "Your room is quite disorganized and messy." (the sandwich ingredient)
3. "You always pride yourself in being such an organized, clean person, so I know you will clean up your room." (the other slice of bread)

You have sandwiched your constructive criticism with praise, which is very different from simply saying, "Holly, your room is a mess. It looks terrible, so clean it up right now!"

Toothpick Exercise

When things are overwhelming for you, take a large handful of toothpicks and drop them so they scatter all over the floor. Then try and pick them up all at once. You will discover this is impossible but if you pick up one, or a few toothpicks at a time, you will be able to complete the task.

Apply this to your life and do what you can, and do not attempt to do everything at the same time. Focus, concentrate and complete your work in sections or parts.

White Light Dome of Protection Exercise

Place a 'White Light Dome of Protection' over your family and you every morning and every night. Some people do it when they are sitting in the car before they start it.

My Experience

I was doing an interview at a radio station in downtown Vancouver in an area referred to as 'Skid Row.' My husband, Reg was driving his little convertible and we arrived a bit early for the interview, so we parked across the street. They had bars on the door of the building, so we had to wait until someone opened the door for us.

As we sat there, we saw all kinds of negative activities, such as shooting-up drugs, etc., and the fear and panic started welling up in me. I started to panic. To make matters even more intense, Reg had developed a severe nose bleed and was sitting in the car with his head back trying to stop the bleeding. Then I remembered my bag of Affirmation Tools and I thought to myself, this is the perfect time to use some of them.

So I immediately placed a special White Light Dome of Protection over Reg and me from the tips of our toes to the roots of our hair and everything and over everyone around us. I also placed a White Light over the little convertible. Then I used another Affirmation Tool, the one where I visualized on the back of my ring these four words, 'This too shall pass,' and it did! Then I stepped ahead in my mind a couple of hours and put myself into the situation of Reg and I being home happy and safe.

Finally they opened the door, we went in and I did my interview. We got some help for Reg's nosebleed so it finally stopped. On the way home, I thought about things. It could have turned out much differently in many ways. I was so happy that I was strong enough to become the Master of my fear and not the servant to it.

Every morning and every evening, I place God's pure White Light (Dome of Protection) over every member of my family and myself from the roots of our hair to the tips of our toes, all day today and every day, all night tonight and every night, and over everything and everyone around us. We are all fully protected! You can use this Dome of Protection any time, especially when you feel threatened. It is a very powerful exercise and works fantastically!

Worry Exercise

Chronic worry is abnormal. A person who worries that he or she has nothing to worry about is a *worry wart!* Worry is such a wasted emotion. The main basis of worry is negativity and apprehension. It could be the expectation that the worst will happen. Tension results from worry and brings on more worry, so that it becomes a vicious circle.

I read somewhere that worry is like a rocking chair — it gives you something to do, but gets you nowhere. It is interest paid on trouble before it becomes due. It is like a boil coming to its painful head — which is fear! Worry becomes fear if you allow it to, or do not control it. And fear short-circuits the cosmic energy that flows throughout your body. It inhibits your cells and creates poison that can be injurious to your organs, tissues, and every part of your body. Any negative thought, if fertilized, can develop into a real fear monster that can tear you down. Conquer fear by putting it into proper perspective. Worrying about things that we cannot control dissipates energy faster than we can accumulate it.

Worry Releasing

Write down everything you are worrying about, date the page, and put it away in a drawer. Then take it out in a year's time and read it. You will discover that 90% of what you worried about never happened and that the 10% that *did* happen was not the least bit affected by your worry. So I ask you, "Why worry?"

Worry Releasing Method

Mentally Accept the Worst that Can Happen in this Situation and Then Immediately Start Improving On It!

When you are worried about something, mentally accept it saying to yourself, "What is the very worst that can happen here?" Then accept the worst mentally. And IMMEDIATELY take steps to improve upon it.

Example of Worry Releasing

I think I have lost my purse. I am panicking and started to immediately search for it.

Then I say to myself, "Stop and mentally accept the fact that I have lost my purse." Then I start to think of ways I can improve upon that situation. I remember that I have all the credit card numbers written down and saved, and photocopies of my Driver's License and all my credit cards. Then my whole body begins to relax, and then I can calmly think of the last place I had my purse and start the search. In most cases, I find what I am looking for in a few minutes. I believe the reason is that when we are worried and frustrated, we cannot think rationally.

Sample Master Affirmation for Handling Fear & Worry

"I, (your name), deserve to be able to and now handle all situations of life. I am confident, calm, safe, and secure. Faith, belief, and confidence radiate from my being. My mind is busy replacing negative thoughts with positive ones. I give myself permission to be happy. I enjoy being free of worry and fear. I believe in myself. I love life and living in the present. I look forward to wonderful things taking place in my life. I am happy, worry-free, and peaceful, to the good of all parties concerned. Thank you, thank you, thank you.

I fully accept"

Signed _____

Dated _____

Address _____

Short Form Affirmation

100% peaceful and worry-free

Affirmations When Properly Done Always Work!

HEALTH & HAPPINESS AFFIRMATION TOOLS

The ABC's of Health

Affirmation Tool
A   **Always**
B   **Be**
C   **Cleansing!**

A

Always accept responsibility for your health. Learn about and understand the full nature of any disease with which you may have been diagnosed. Always be conscious of what you can do to assist your body in cleansing, healing, and revitalizing.

B

Be yourself. Never attempt to copy others. You are unique. Believe disease can be cured and be willing to explore various avenues of healing. Listen to the advice of your healthcare practitioner and other well-meaning people. After careful consideration, make your own decisions. The internet is a great source of valuable information about virtually every subject.

C

Cleanse your mind, emotions, and body of harmful drugs, negative thoughts, emotions, or chemicals. Drugs, pre-scribed or otherwise, act as poisons in your system. Toxins form a part of every chronic, degenerative disease.

Body Clock Programmed to Wake Up at Certain Time

When you wish to be awakened at a certain hour, use your subconscious mind as our alarm clock. Just before going to sleep, tell your subconscious mind to awaken you at a specific time. I use this exercise often; it never ceases to amaze me that I wake up exactly at the time specified.

Its accuracy is not affected by the change of time or the clock being slow.

Say often during the day, "I am whole, perfect, strong, powerful, loving, harmonious, happy, healthy and peaceful."

Happiness – An Inside Job

Claim Your Birthright of Health, Love, Happiness & Prosperity NOW!

True happiness comes from within. It is an inside job! I feel you are experiencing happiness when you are happy with who you are, what you are doing and who you are doing it with.

Yes, a wonderful spouse, family, home, car and material things can and do ADD to your happiness, but know that real, true happiness starts within you!

Say often during the day--"Today I am happy, fulfilled and loved."

Whistle or hum a little upbeat tune. Step into your circle of happiness starting right here and right now!

It is your birthright to be healthy, happy, loved and prosperous.

Internal Boil Release Exercise

Stop swallowing negativity. When someone says something mean or negative to you, refuse to allow it to enter into your subconscious (computer). Say, "Stop, you are not welcome; you cannot enter into my mind or being!" Then say, "I am happy, healthy and fulfilled." The danger of not standing up for yourself or accepting other's negative comments and action is that you stifle these emotions and then when you least expect it, they will erupt without notice.

I feel it is best to not allow them to enter your body, take up residency, fester and become Internal Boils. I know I have experienced the eruption of some of those Internal Boils, and it was not a happy experience.

Master Affirmation to be Healthy
Permission to be Healthy Agreement

"I, (your name), hereby give myself permission to be 100% healthy. I deserve create, and have health and happiness in my life. I believe in myself and my abilities. I am safe and protected. I enjoy doing my Affirmations regularly. I take responsibility for learning more about my body and my health. I seek out and employ ways to improve my health daily. I enjoy relaxing, meditating, and exercising. I love myself unconditionally. I accept and approve of myself. I allow myself to be me. I am whole, perfect, strong, powerful, loving, harmonious, and happy, to the good of all parties concerned. Thank you, thank you, thank you.

I fully accept"

Signed _____

Dated _____

Address _____

When you sign your name, you say, "Yes, I validate, accept and agree with this permission slip. I am aware that no one else has a signature just like mine." You have just created a firm and binding document with your Higher Self, God/Creator, Universal Mind or whomever you believe in.

Affirmations When Properly Done Always Work!

LOVE AFFIRMATION TOOLS

3 Important Aspects of Love

Affirmation Tool

1st Aspect -- LOVABLE

The 1st and most important aspect of love is that of being *lovable*. There must be love from self to self before it can be extended to others. You cannot give from an empty cup. Fill your cup of divine self-love to overflowing. You are lovable in spite of any shortcomings and faults. Learn to love your individuality and your connection with God.

2nd Aspect -- LOVING

The 2nd aspect of love is that of *loving*, whereby you give and express love to others and self. Loving others comes naturally and easily when you fully love yourself.

3rd Aspect -- LOVED

The 3rd aspect of love is that of *being loved*. You need to allow yourself to be loved and to fully receive love from others.

If you strive daily to achieve these three states, you will come to understand the true meaning of unconditional love. To achieve unconditional love in your life, all three of these aspects must be happening simultaneously.

Everyone needs love—no matter how independent, wealthy, or successful a person may be. Without love, there is no self-actualization. Love is an element as essential to our well-being as air or water.

When you have all three of these, you are now in a better position to teach love and respect to your children.

Give Love and Teach Your Children How to Have and Enjoy a Healthy Self-Love

Teach your child or children to have a healthy love and respect of self. It is also important to teach them to be kind, caring and to respect others as well. You do not want your child to grow up to be selfish with the 'Me, Me Syndrome,' where everything, and I mean everything, is about him or her.

When children love, respect and approve of themselves, the need for bullying and having control over others disappears, as they are content within themselves. We, as parents, need to teach our children from a very young age loving kindness to self and others.

Teach Your Children Self-Love Exercise

Teach your child to look into the mirror and say, "Hey, self you are a great kid. I now let go of my negative, sad and disappointed feelings. I love, respect and approve of myself. I like and respect others and treat everyone with kindness."

Instruct them on the dangers of taking rides from people without your permission, doing drugs, smoking or drinking alcohol. Also encourage them to walk in groups for safety. Again, there is a fine line between scaring our children and informing them of safety measures. Be involved in your child's life and interact with their day care, and schools.

Affirmation Light Bulb for Family

You may wish to do your family Affirmations in a special place, such as a garden, meadow, arbour, or anywhere you and your family feel comfortable and at peace. I enjoy doing my Affirmation Program in my own mental Affirmation Light Bulb which helps make my Affirmations more focused and powerful.

To do this, visualize a huge, giant light bulb in front of you. Make it large enough for your whole family to step inside. It is complete with door and handle. Open the glass door and go inside. You can see through it in all directions. Just inside the door, there is a panel of push buttons.

When you are working creating harmonious family relationships and situations, press the pink button. This color will then fill your Affirmation Light Bulb, penetrating the atmosphere and enabling everyone to breathe in the power of that specific color. When doing an Affirmation for money for a family vacation, use the color green as green represents money and abundance.

Imagine putting your Family Affirmation into a soft, golden cloud and letting it float up and out the large fresh air vent at the top of the Affirmation Light Bulb. Release it with loving kindness and detachment into the Universe, to manifest as desired.

Now mentally harden the material around the bulb so that no one else can come in for this time.

Bring in the 5 senses.

SEE	a huge wicker chair, covered with large colored pillows in gorgeous pastel colors
HEAR	soothing music---Sit down in the chair
FEEL	your body sink into deep relaxation

SMELL   the sweet fragrance of roses
TASTE   *pop a* mint into your mouth to complete the experience of the five senses

Love Magnet

Repeat over and over, "I am a LOVE MAGNET, to the right people and right situations."

Unselfish, healthy love is healing and self-assuring. All love begins with self-love. Loving self, as you are, gives you the permission and the ability to change. Acceptance is the highest form of love. Practicing acceptance in your daily life enables you and others to be themselves. On the other hand, envying others or comparing yourself to them inhibits self-love and acceptance.

My Story

When I first learned about being a 'Love Magnet,' I put it into effect. When I was running a Motel in Deserve Hot Springs every morning I went for my early morning walk. As I walked along, I kept repeating to myself over and over, "I am a love magnet." I was so caught up in my Affirmations that I did not notice a dog that ran up to me. I just looked at the dog and said, "I'm a love magnet." He kind of looked at me and wagged his tail. His owner came running up, out of breath and said, "Are you okay? This is a vicious dog you know and he just broke his chain." I smiled and said, "I 'm a love magnet." He muttered something under his breath, shook his head and walked away. Now, since that time I have learned to say, "I am a love magnet to the right people and circumstances." It is very important when learning these Affirmation Tools to learn about how to put it into effect in its entirety.

154

Sample Master Affirmation for Love

"I am lovable, loving and loved. I love, respect and approve of myself just the way I am. I have and enjoy great, healthy self-respect and self-worth. I am a powerful Love Magnet to the right people and right situations. I am happy, and full of love to the good of all parties concerned. Thank you, thank you thank you.

I fully accept"

Signed _____

Dated _____

Address _____

Affirmations When Properly Done Always Work!

MEDITATION AFFIRMATION TOOLS

PEACE OF MIND

How do you find Peace by Meditation? Peace of mind is a state of mind. It is not something you acquire, but something you express. It does not come from what you get but how you use what you have. Peace is the condition of mind and body that you reach when you are satisfied with the thoughts you are thinking, the life you are living, and the things you are doing. Peace is the state of your mind when your thoughts are still. It is completeness, totality, awareness, and spiritual growth.

Some people can relax by playing music. Do whatever works for you. Tell yourself you will return in twenty minutes, refreshed and full of radiant energy. Setting your own time limit is important so that your subconscious mind will ensure that you observe it.

Take several deep breaths, breathing out all negative thoughts, worries, and cares. Then breathe in happy thoughts of peace, joy, love, and happiness.

Meditation Process

Meditation is an effort made on the part of the conscious mind to close the gap between itself and the subconscious mind. Meditation is simply a quiet state of mind, a silence of thought. The growth of living things and the movement of the heavens are silent. The dictionary defines meditation — 'to ponder or to engage in continuous and contemplative thought.' Take fifteen to twenty minutes from your busy day in the morning and late afternoon or evening to meditate.

Find a quiet spot

Sit or lie down

Relax and clear your mind

Tell yourself that you will be back in twenty minutes

Concentrate on one two-syllable word to help you focus. If you desire peace, concentrate on the word *peaceful* and keep repeating it over and over in your mind.

If you desire love, concentrate on the word *loving*. Keep repeating this one word over and over, to the exclusion of all other thoughts, ideas, and words. Feel yourself going deeper and deeper into relaxation. Find that quiet space within where the real you resides. Let yourself go completely. Tell yourself that you will return in 20 minutes. Enjoy the meditation and then come back to reality fresh, healthy and happy.

Meditation to Increase Your Self-Esteem

Sit quietly every morning for thirty to thirty-five minutes and mentally forgive *everyone* and *everything* that has ever hurt you. Then mentally ask for forgiveness for your negative, hurtful thoughts, feelings, and actions to self and others.

If you have criticized or gossiped about anyone, withdraw those negative words, thoughts, and feelings by asking for forgiveness. See everyone as spirit and send them your strongest, purest, highest quality of love.

Release and let go of hurt from others to achieve peace of mind, love of self and spiritual growth. You need to take responsibility for your own health, body, and life.

Love yourself and your life. It is the only one you have. Tell yourself you are a wonderful, worthwhile human being and that no one can keep God's blessings from you.

Find a comfortable place to sit or lie down, one where you will not be disturbed. Wear comfortable clothes. Clear your mind of all cares, worries and endless thoughts. Just allow yourself to BE. Now you are ready to embark on your incredible, wondrous journey into self-discovery and self-realization, a world that only YOU can discover. You truly enjoy this wonderful, safe space of total relaxation! Feel yourself drifting into a state of total peace and relaxation. Gently close your eyes.

Let's Begin

With your eyes closed, take my hand and I will lead you to the top of the 3 steps that will take you down into deep meditation. These steps are covered in pure velvet so you can take off your shoes and go in your bare feet if you wish.

1ˢᵗ Step

You are so safe and becoming more and more relaxed. You are excited and enthusiastic about this journey.

2ⁿᵈ Step

Down deeper, deeper into relaxation and still so safe and protected and peaceful. Your body is a little numb and so-o-o relaxed you just don't feel like moving it.

3ʳᵈ Step

Take this last step that puts you onto a soft, glistening carpet of grass. You have arrived. Look around you at the beautiful garden of s, flowers, trees and God's creations.

Look — Look over there – There is the River of Self-Esteem with its beautiful pink water. See the Angel of Self-Esteem. She hands you some carving tools and motions you to a large block of ice and encourages you to carve out the perfect YOU!

The Angel of Self-Esteem has a lovely picture of you, looking radiantly happy, peaceful and full of self-confidence. She leaves this picture by the block of ice and fades into the background.

It is your choice to leave it there or to pick it up and use it as a guide when chiseling the perfect YOU out of the block of ice. When you have finished your carving and your image is exactly what you wish it to be, then go to the river and take a container from the bank and fill it with the Magical pink water of self-esteem.

Holding the picture in your hand that the Angel of Self-Esteem gave you, you softly whisper *"Thank you, thank you, thank you,"* to that beautiful Angel for your miracle.

A h h h ………….. Just take a moment or two to be quiet and totally allow these happy, positive feelings to sink deep into your subconscious mind, where they will take root, grow and become reality in your Life. Know that you will never be in the state of not loving, respecting and approving of yourself again. You are totally lovable, loved and loving. You are filled to the brim with healthy self-respect, self-esteem and self-worth.

You DESERVE that happy, lasting, loving relationship. You are truly amazed at how great you feel. In this state of total relaxation, allow these words to saturate your entire body--"I am loving, loved and lovable. I am love!"

Pause for a second of two. You feel so light and comfortable in your body. Now start your short journey home, back up the stairs you came down.

3rd Step

Going up, still relaxed and peaceful. You are feeling more and more relaxed and peaceful as the time goes by.

2nd Step

Going up still another step. You really don't want to leave this truly magical and healing place, but you know you have to go back to reality.

1st Step

You have arrived. You take a deep breath and breathe in the fresh brisk air. You will never, ever doubt yourself again or feel that you are inferior to others. Your self-love and self-respect are growing by leaps and bounds daily.

You have the picture of yourself looking so happy and self-confident. Any 'so-called' mistakes from the past are just that—past, completely forgotten! You know there is no right or wrong way, only the chosen way. Use any 'so-called' mistakes as extraordinary fertilizer for your present and coming successes.

You can feel your self-confidence level rising. You feel totally wonderful. This healing power is surging throughout your body. You feel so relaxed and comforted. You are so happy and excited.

At the count of 3 you will become wide awake, happy and excited to go on about your everyday life.

1. Open your eyes and look around
2. Become aware of where you are
3. You are wide awake, excited and full of enthusiasm and expectancy

And Knowing That Affirmations When Properly Done Always Work!

The good news is that you can go back to visit anytime you wish, just play this Meditation and it will bring back all the memories. Each time you go on the meditation it will be different--at times more in depth, sometimes more serious and other times full of fun and laughter.

You have your Magic Self-Esteem Wand, your Trigger Tool to make your Affirmation Meditation a reality. You have taken your Affirmation out of the unreal (the unknown), and placed it into the real (the known) by participating in this Self-Esteem Meditation.

You already have that radiant self-confidence and it is appearing in your reality.

Now say, *"Thank you, thank you, thank you,"* and live in an attitude of gratitude and be open, accept and receive your completed Self-Esteem Affirmation. **Act as if** you are already that person full of self-confidence, health and happiness. It is yours! Step into it. After this Meditation, you will never be the same. All worry, concern and frustration about not being good enough or not able to do the things you want to do have gone. It evaporated, as if by magic. You KNOW you DESERVE and now have that lasting, loving relationship with the perfect life partner for you.

Sample Master Affirmation for Spiri]tual Growth

"I, (your name), now open up to and deserve higher levels of awareness. I am safe. I now meditate on all that is good, kind, and peaceful. All negativity and fear leave my body now. I attract peace, goodness, and harmony. My mind is free from worry because I am in direct contact with the source of God's power and intelligence. This enables me to dissolve the cause of worry. I am calm and handle any situation. I am free of fear and worry. Spiritual awakening is penetrating every cell, muscle, tissue, and every part of my being. I believe in myself and my life. I experience new levels of spirituality, tranquility, love, peace, and joy. I am happy, to the good of all parties concerned. Thank you, thank you, thank you.

I fully accept"

Signed _____

Dated _____

Address _____

Affirmations When Properly Done Always Work!

MONEY AFFIRMATION TOOLS

Act 'As If'

This is an exercise created to help you develop and increase your prosperity consciousness. Select a high end restaurant or hotel in your area. Dress up in your best clothes and go there. Bring in your 5 physical senses. **See** the beautiful, expensive, lavish surroundings and the elegantly dressed people; Smell the wonderful smell of fresh apple pie; Hear the waitperson asking to take your order. Order tea &/or coffee and a very expensive lunch or dessert. Feel how prosperous you feel as you sink into the deep cushioned chair.

When your order arrives, enjoy the **taste** of that delicious food. Know that you can come back, in your mind, whenever you please to experience this wonderful sensation and feeling of prosperity. Whisper to yourself, "This must be what it feels like to have a lot of money and spend it as you wish."

The feelings of a wealthy person penetrate into your subconscious mind and you KNOW that money is on its way to you. Know that you will always have the feeling of abundance of money and prosperity in your life.

Affirmation Light Bulb for Money

You may wish to do your *Affirmation Process* in a special place, such as a garden, meadow, tree house, arbor, or anywhere you feel comfortable and at peace. I enjoy doing my

Affirmation Program in my own mental Affirmation Light Bulb which helps make my Affirmations more focused and powerful.

To do this, visualize a huge light bulb in front of you. Make it large enough to step inside. It is complete with door and handle. Open the glass door and go inside. You can see through it in all directions. Just inside the door there is a panel of push buttons.

When you are working on attracting money, press the green button. This green color you selected will then fill your Affirmation Light Bulb, penetrating the atmosphere and enabling you to breathe in the power of that specific color. Green represents change, growth, and money.

Imagine putting your money Affirmation in a soft, golden cloud and letting it float up and out the large fresh air vent at the top of the Affirmation Light Bulb. Release it with loving kindness and detachment into the Universe, to manifest as desired.

Now mentally harden the material around the bulb so that no one can come in or see you.

Bring in your 5 senses.

SEE	a huge wicker chair covered with large colored pillows in gorgeous pastel colors
HEAR	soothing music---Sit down in the chair
FEEL	your body sink into deep relaxation
SMELL	the sweet fragrance of roses
TASTE	a tasty mint in your mouth to complete the experience of the five senses

I use this valuable exercise for a positive pick-me-up whenever I begin to feel discouraged or disheartened or when I need to manifest money. I sit, meditate, and ask for new, fresh ideas. When you do your Affirmation

Process in this wonderful space, it helps solidify, clarify, and empower your Affirmations.

Create your very own peaceful place. It is a good idea to keep your own individual light-bulb space just for you. This is your secret place. Create whatever you desire. Make it special, unique, and completely safe. Allow your imagination and creative visualization abilities to run wild!

Planting a Tiny Angel Pin

This can by a great Affirmation Tool to help you sell your property easily and quickly. Plant a tiny Angel Pin (face up) in the ground around the house/property that you want to sell. As you gently place it into the ground say, "Dear Angel, Please help me sell my house/property at the perfect price, to the perfect people at the perfect time. Thank you, thank you, thank you."

Many readers have reported great success using this simple Affirmation Tool.

My Planting Story

I had just put my house on the market and was desirous of selling it quickly. At the time, the market in that particular area was very slow. Some of the houses had been on the market for the past three years and still had not sold.

When a friend told me about the process of planting a miniature statue of a saint or   Angel in your front yard to sell your house quickly, I decided to do this exercise using a tiny Angel metal pin. I gently placed the Angel, which I named the Angel of Prosperity, in the ground in my front yard. I thanked the Angel for helping me sell my house quickly and easily to the good of all parties concerned. Three weeks after I had planted the Angel pin I had an acceptable offer. It really did work!

This is a great Affirmation Tool to quickly and easily help you sell your home. Many readers have reported great success using this method. Plant a tiny Angel in your front yard to magnetize money to you or to help you sell your property. When planting the tiny Angel pin, be sure and plant the Angel face-up.

Bank Statement

This is a very simple, easy and yet highly effective exercise to manifest the exact amount of money you desire.

Take a photocopy of your bank statement. On the photocopy, white out the amount printed there and put in the amount you *wish* to see there. This gives your subconscious mind a figure upon which to focus which you desire.

Big Money to Me Now

First of all determine just what 'Big Money' means for you.

Do this exercise in front of the window so you can magnetize the power from God, Universal Mind or whomever you believe in, the sun, moon, stars and the entire Universe into your Magic Magnetic Circle. What you are affirming for yourself, affirm that for all others as well.

Stand up and stretch your arms out as far as you can and say, 'Big' *with* your right hand, draw an imaginary $ sign in the air saying, 'Money.' With both hands parallel, make two downward lines to complete the dollar sign.

Now say "To me now," as you tap your heart area with your right hand. With hands cupped in the prayer position bow three times i.e. to the left, then the middle and right saying: "Thank you, thank you, thank you."

Bypass Money – Go Directly to Desired Object

On occasion you may wish to do what I do. Sometimes I bypass the money and affirm for what I would purchase or do with the actual cash. I have used this method many times with astounding results. It just blew me away!

Do this, as an added exercise during the day and it will help you feel, live, and experience the prosperity consciousness.

When I decided I wanted a new car, I bypassed the money and went directly into a Master Affirmation to attract that new car into my life. I affirmed as follows:

"I, Anne Marie Evers, deserve and now have the car of my choice in excellent condition. It is all paid for. I am safe and protected in my car to the good of all parties concerned. Thank you, thank you, thank you."

(I used the words 'car of my choice' because I kept changing my mind as to what kind of a vehicle I wanted.)

My Affirmation manifested as affirmed. My fiancé gave me a new car as a pre-wedding gift. When driving it home from the dealership, he asked me how it felt driving my brand new car. I replied, "Oh, just like always." He said, "You have never driven this car before." I said, "Oh yes, I have, many, many times in my mind." The mind does not know the difference between a real and an imagined event and takes it as the truth and acts upon it. It is so important to live in an attitude of gratitude and focus on and be thankful for the good things that we have in our lives and for the good that is coming to us.

Check Writing Exercise

This Affirmation Tool encourages you to expand your money consciousness by doing the step process. Should you have problems believing you could receive the sum of $1,000,000, increase your ability to believe step-by- step.

Write yourself a check first for $100, then $1000, then $10,000, then $100,000. When your belief system is strong enough and you have developed prosperity conscious- ness, write yourself that check for $1,000,000! No need to stop there.

Carry this check with you at all times. Look at it often and bless it. Thank it for materializing.

Doodle Dollar Signs

This simple and easy exercise brings your money consciousness to the front burner of your mind and cre- ates a feeling of abundance. When you *doodle*, write dol- lar signs *$$$$$$$$*; you create and develop your money consciousness.

Fold Your Money

This is one way of working smarter, not harder.

Fold your paper money in half, face up towards you. Never fold your paper money in half from the back of the bill. If you do, you will experience money draining away from you. One of my students did the Fold Your Money Exercise with the money facing up and was amazed and thrilled to find $2,000.00 in an old dresser he was refinishing.

Honey on Bathing Suit Exercise

This is what I refer to as the *Money Sticking Exercise.*

My sister Darlene was complaining that no matter how much money she and her husband brought into the home, there was never enough. It went out faster than it came in. She devised the following exercise which helped her immensely and in her words, "It saved us from bankruptcy."

She put on her bathing suit and smeared some honey on it in various places. Then she took paper money and stuck it to her. She had her picture taken in her *Honey Money Bathing Suit* doing her Money Sticking Exercise.

She used this as a visual, and her subconscious mind got the message and she was amazed at how her life changed for the better. No, they did not bring in more money monthly, but somehow it stayed with them. They were both very surprised.

Money on the Ceiling Exercise

Place paper bills (money) on your ceiling in your bedroom, or whatever room you choose. If you wish, you can use monopoly money or put dollar amounts on pieces of paper and thumbtack or pin them to your ceiling. The reason this works is that you are increasing and expanding your money consciousness by visually seeing it just before you go to sleep and just as soon as you wake up. This is the time that your mind is in its most receptive state to receive instructions.

Another option is to have a cork bulletin board to thumbtack or pin money on. Make it very visible in your bedroom or other room so that it is the first thing you see when you wake up.

My Own Experience with the Money on the Ceiling Exercise

Many years ago, before I even knew what an Affirmation was, I was doing one—perhaps the most important Affirmation of my life. My son David was born with two severely crooked feet. His feet were so turned in that he could not walk. We were very poor and it would have taken several thousand dollars for corrective surgery to enable him to walk. To everyone, he seemed doomed to live his life in a wheelchair.

I looked at my baby son and I said over and over, "You will walk, you will walk." I repeated this statement dozens of times every day and lulled myself to sleep at night, saying, "David will walk, David will walk!" It was my intention that he would walk and I commanded it.

I teach in my books and workshops that we always need to affirm in the *now* and not say *will*. However, at that time I said to my son, "You will walk." That was a decree or command and even though I put it off into the future, it worked. At that time in my life I had not even heard of Affirmations. Shortly thereafter, a friend introduced me to a wonderful organization (Shriners) that paid for my son's corrective surgery and hospitalization in Portland, Oregon.

At the time, when David was released from the hospital, we had a restaurant in Cranbrook, B.C. One day while David was sitting in his highchair in the restaurant wearing clumsy, corrective shoes, a customer said to me, "What is wrong with the little guy?." I told him the story about my son's crooked feet and how the Shriners had helped us.

When he left, he gave me a generous tip. Under his business card on the table was a $10.00 bill. He had scribbled on his business card, "This is for the little guy." My husband, Al, took the $10.00 bill, and with a thumbtack he put both the business card and the money on the ceiling. I was wondering what he was doing, but when the next customer came in and said, "What is that money doing on the ceiling?" I told him the story and, sure enough, when he left he also left a generous tip with his business card.

This went on day after day. When people did not have a business card, Al simply took one of our restaurant business cards and placed it with the money on the ceiling. Before long, we had hundreds of dollars on the ceiling. People came from miles away just to see the money on the ceiling, and it is interesting to note that our business started to flourish and we were becoming very prosperous. When we finally sold the Steak House, we had thousands of dollars on the ceiling, which was donated to the Shriners Hospital. The money on the ceiling created a powerful money consciousness for us, our business, and our customers that was absolute proof that the Law of Attraction works!

Money Safe

Visualize in your mind's eye a huge money safe with your name on it. See it overflowing with money. Now see yourself getting the right combination and opening it. How do you feel? Take out as much money as you desire. There is no lack in this safe, and as soon as you take out an amount, it is automatically replaced with even more.

It is your responsibility to create your own beliefs about prosperity and let go of any negative beliefs you may have picked up along the way.

Congratulations--You are now inducted into the Multi-Millionaire's Hall of Fame. You will spend your wealth wisely and use a portion of it to help those in need. You are now happy, fulfilled and at peace to the good of all parties concerned.

Money Schedule – Time Frame Circles

Never become discouraged if your Affirmation does not work instantly. It could take time, and each time you do these exercises you increase your faith.

Doing these exercises brings the prosperity consciousness into your being, personality, life, and world.

Almost everyone I meet is excited to find out *When – When--When!* When is it going to manifest? To get an answer from your subconscious mind as to approximately when your Affirmation will manifest, do the following procedure in your mind.

Close your eyes. Visualize in your mind's eye four circles –

First circle says *immediately*
Second circle says *six months*
Third circle says **12 months** *or one year*
Fourth circle says *other*

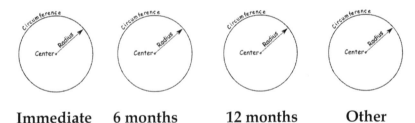

Immediate   6 months   12 months   Other

Mentally think of the amount of money that you desire and then watch it go into one circle. Don't send it or force it. Just allow it to go in on its own. This process works best if you allow yourself to be the silent observer, *simply watching* it going into one of the circles.

If it does not want to go into any circle, do the process again or wait for a while, as your subconscious mind may not be ready to answer.

Money Shower

When you get up in the morning and when you are taking your shower, stand under the water and ask it to cleanse your entire body of any negative thoughts, beliefs, and ideas that you are not good enough to have and enjoy being rich. Allow the power of forgiveness of all past negative thoughts, beliefs, and events concerning the lack of money to flow through every cell of your body.

Say, "I, (your name), now forgive everyone and everything that has EVER hurt me. I now forgive myself. I love, respect, and approve of myself just the way I am. I forgive myself for not managing my money more carefully, for any negative situation where I lost money," etc. Feel *every* cell of your body being filled with pure forgiveness.

After you feel that the water has washed away every speck of negativity, hurt, and disappointment, then visualize the water pouring over you from the roots of your hair to the tips of your toes with feelings of unconditional love, respect, and approval. Then turn off the shower and as you dry yourself off, affirm gently and lovingly to your body —

"Body, you are the greatest and you deserve the very best. I love, respect, and approve of you just the way you are. You deserve and now have and enjoy abundant wealth, health, and happiness. Thank you, thank you, thank you. I fully accept." Then get dressed and go about your day. Now you have released all thoughts of not being good enough, not deserving, etc., and you have opened the door for that great wealth to flow into your life. It is a wonderful idea to dedicate the positive flow of water to people worldwide in need of water. Before I step into my bath, I always dedicate the water to people needing water.

Money Under Your Pillow Exercise

Place paper money under your pillow at night and ask that it multiply for you. This way your subconscious mind has all night to go out and assemble conditions to bring that prosperity to you. Lull yourself to sleep saying, "Great wealth, great wealth."

Money Tree Exercise

The following exercise can be very powerful in helping you manifest abundance in your life. Purchase a small tree and plant it in your backyard. If you are limited for space, plant a small tree in a pot in your home, or make one from material. Place paper money bills on it, using clothespins or paperclips to attach the bills to the branches or leaves.

If you are unable to do it with real money, take pieces of paper and write out the amounts you wish to see multiplied: $50, $100, $5,000, $100,000, or more. You can also use *Monopoly* money. Alternatively, you may visualize your own money tree. *See* yourself picking all the money you desire—$10s, $20s, $50s, $100s, $1,000s—from your very own money tree. *Bring in all 5 senses.*

You will find a money tree in my home. I find it great for borrowing money and, when I replace it, I always add at least five dollars for the earned interest. You will find that opportunities you never dreamed were possible will come to you. You will be offered positions or business opportunities that will make money for you. New ideas will come to you from your subconscious as you hold the thought of prosperity firmly in your mind.

Prosperity Map

Take a huge piece of chart paper and draw a giant circle as big as you can on it. Then draw another small circle in the middle and put your photograph in that circle. *(I always place the Angel of Wealth there as well.)*

Draw clouds and then write all the things you desire regarding money and prosperity on pieces of sticky paper. Place these into the cloud spaces. Then take a pencil or pen, and with a line going from each of your desires, connect them to the inner circle where your picture is.

Know that you are drawing and magnetizing all these desires to you through the Law of Attraction, which states, "Like attracts like; more gathers more; what you think about you bring about; and what you are seeking is seeking you."

Here are some of the things I have written on my Prosperity Map

> "I have and enjoy loving harmonious relationships with my spouse and all family members; my spiritual growth is always increasing to higher levels; all my books are sold; I have in excess of 10 paying clients weekly; new prosperity ideas come to me daily; I have many good friends; I have a new car; my house is paid for; I pay all my bills promptly

and on time; people that owe me money repay me; my Cards of Life are all sold; My family and I all have and enjoy abundant health; I have extra money to help others; I love life. "

Try it! Write whatever you like. Remember that you should be realistic and have the faith and belief that what you are affirming manifests as affirmed.

Attach an envelope to the bottom of the chart that says, 'Completed Affirmations.' When one of your desires manifests, put a huge checkmark through it, then take it off the place where the cloud drawing is and put it into the Completed Affirmations envelope which you have attached to the bottom of the chart. This, of course, increases your faith.

This way there is always room to add more and more desires.

On the bottom of the chart paper write:

"I fully accept.

To the good of all parties concerned thank you, thank you, thank you!"

Signed_____

Dated _____

Prosperity Party

Have a prosperity party where you invite your friends. Make everything about prosperity. Have $ napkins, dollar signs on the paper plates and cups. Also have huge dollar signs hanging from the ceiling. Talk about prosperity--what does it mean to each person, ways of making money, etc.

Prosperity Tape Exercise

Prosperity tapes are fun to make and you can use any wording you desire. You can put music to your Affirmations and sing little catchy tunes.

Make up your own prosperity tape using your own voice, since that's the voice your subconscious mind is most in tune with.

Salt Exercise

You may wish to experiment with this fun and effective salt exercise. I put a light dab of honey on my paper money and I sprinkle salt on it, saying, "Salt, please purify; salt, please multiply." I usually keep this particular money in a safe place and somewhere where it will not become stuck to my other paper money.

Salt Exercise Testimonial

Florence, one of my readers, reported that she had been experiencing fabulous results with the Salt Exercise. She purchased a brand new container of salt. She says it must be salt that has never been opened before. She takes her paper money and sprinkles it with this salt. She closes her eyes and says, "Please purify and multiply this money for me now. Thank you, thank you, thank you." Then she tosses a pinch of salt over her left shoulder. She says she used to return almost everything she purchased, but since doing this exercise (cleaning her money) she says she is drawn to only purchasing things that she really wants.

She also says her money actually goes much farther. She is convinced that it works!

Saving Money for Your Retirement

Put as much money as you can into a Savings Plan, Retirement Fund, etc. Be consistent. Even if you start with a small amount, over time it builds up for that important "nest egg." when you reach retirement.

Sample Master Affirmation for Picking from Your Own Money Tree

"I, (your name), deserve to have and now easily pick from my very own money tree in my backyard the sum of $_____ (net/gross) to pay my immediate debts and to use for spending money. I am not concerned about how this happens. I simply release this request with faith and expectancy into the Universe. Divine Intelligence now puts this money into my hands or my bank account. The power of my subconscious mind now brings it to pass in its own way. I get out of the way and allow it to manifest. I am content and happy, to the good of all parties concerned. Thank you, thank you, thank you.

I fully accept"

Signed_____

Dated _____

Address _____

Affirmations When Properly Done Always Work!

OVERWHELMED AFFIRMATION TOOLS

When you are feeling overwhelmed, give it up to God/ Creator or whomever you believe in.

Hourglass

When I am overwhelmed, thinking "How can I ever get everything done that I need to do today?" I do the Hourglass Exercise. I have an hourglass on my desk close to my computer. I watch each grain of sand going through the neck of the hourglass and think about how just one grain of sand is able to get through at a time. If I try to force more than one grain, it clogs up and stops. I use this in my life, doing only one task at one time, and that way everything gets done.

A similar analogy would be eating an apple. If you tried to eat an apple *whole*, you would choke or would not be able to accomplish the task of eating the apple. However if you cut it up into bite size pieces you could then eat and enjoy the apple. Don't try to tackle a huge project at once!

Percentage %

I used this process all the time. When I am writing my book, articles, columns and writings, I calculate that I am __% finished. This really helps me stay focused as I know I am making progress. Try it and see how it works for you.

Serenity Prayer

God grant me the serenity
To accept the things I cannot change
The courage to change the things I can
And grant the wisdom to know the difference
Apply this to your life and do what you can and do not attempt to do everything at the same time. Focus, concentrate and complete your work in sections or parts.

Things are not as They Seem - The Deal that Wooden Go Through

I was a co-owner of a real estate company in Sumas, Washington State. One day a man named Jeff came into the office and said he was a realtor and wanted a position selling real estate for the company. He said that he had a wooden leg and sometimes he had to lay down on the floor and adjust it. I asked him if that would in any way hinder him from selling real estate and he said, "No, it wouldn't be a problem." One day, I had a phone call from a lady in California inquiring about real estate in our area. She had heard that the property was beautiful, very reasonably priced and a great place to raise her children. Just then Jeff came into the office and immediately laid down on the floor and started to adjust his wooden leg. First he moaned in pain, and when he adjusted his wooden leg to a comfortable position for him, all of a sudden he said in a rather loud voice, "Oh, oh, A h h, oh that feels so good!" The 'wood be' customer at the other end of the phone said, "What's going on up there? Are you having a sex orgy or what?" "No," I answered, "My salesman, Jeff, has a wooden leg and he is lying on the floor adjusting it to a comfortable position for him." She exclaimed, "Humph! A likely story," and she hung up. She never called back!

This Too Shall Pass

This is a very important and helpful exercise. I use it often and rely on it as one of my wonderful Affirmation Tools. When I am in an uncomfortable and/or negative situation, I simply visualize on the back of my ring these four words, "This too shall pass," and it does, together with the good times. This is what we call life. I really see in my mind's eye these four words and receive power and comfort from them.

Toothpick

When things are overwhelming for you, take a large handful of toothpicks and drop them so they scatter all over the floor. Then try and pick them all up at once. You will discover this is impossible, but if you pick up one or a few toothpicks at a time, you will be able to complete the task. Apply this to your life and do what you can, and do not attempt to do everything at the same time. Focus, concentrate and complete your work in sections or parts.

Sample Master Affirmation for Feeling Overwhelmed

"I, (your name), deserve and now am calm and peaceful. I do one task at a time and complete it. When I feel overwhelmed, I say to myself, "One grain of sand at a time," as I watch the sand in my hourglass sitting on my desk. I am happy, organized and peaceful to the good of all parties concerned. Thank you, thank you, thank you.

I fully accept."

Signed_____

Dated _____

Address _____

Affirmations When Properly Done Always Work!

RELATIONSHIP AFFIRMATION TOOLS

10 Seconds of Silence

In every relationship, we have it is important to use the 10 Seconds of Silence Affirmation Tool. This gives cooling off time in disagreements, time to think and gather thoughts.

10 Magic Words That Changed Her Life

Do you want to be more popular and liked? If so, talk in the other person's interest.

Say, "You are so interesting please tell me all about yourself."

When Deanna came to see me she was very unhappy. She was desperate to find out how to become popular, especially as she had no dates and her friends were always dating. I thought about it and then I remembered a situation in my life. I was acting as journalist and was asked to write a story on a very busy, famous millionaire. When I arrived at his office, he said very firmly, "I only have fifteen minutes to give you, and then I have an important meeting." I agreed and we got started.

I asked him all about himself. I said, "Peter, you are so interesting. Tell me about yourself." Well he did! And one hour and a half later, I stood up and said, "Excuse me, Peter, but I do have another appointment." I thought about this later and wondered to myself why he made such a point of telling me about the fifteen minute time period and then gave me an hour and half. Then it dawned on me! Of course, he was talking about the most important person in his Universe (him) and on that there was no time limit! I shared this story with Deanna and her eyes sparkled as she left my office. Did it work? Of course it did, and now she has so many dates her friends are asking her what is her secret!

Affirmation Light Bulb for Relationships

Invite your partner to participate in this exercise, making a private space together. This can be very romantic, exciting, and fulfilling. One couple who made their own mental Marriage Affirmation Light Bulb swears it saved their marriage. They used it as a safe and sacred place in which to settle disagreements, make love, and talk openly about their feelings. They had a place to run away to, even if it was only in their minds. The whole procedure was very real to them. They incorporated creative visualization, imagination, and reality. Now that they are in a better financial position, they do the same exercise on the physical plane, joking that their expensive hotel room is their very own mental Marriage Affirmation Light Bulb.
To recap the importance of L O V E

3 Important Aspects of Love

Check to see how you rate in these 3 Aspects of Love. Are you lovable? Are you loving? Are you loved? If not, do the following Master Affirmation.

Sample Master Affirmation for Self-Love

"I, (your name), deserve and have love, respect and approve of myself. I have and enjoy great healthy self-respect and am self-confident. I am lovable, loving and loved. I am happy to the good of all parties concerned. Thank you, thank you, thank you.

I fully accept"

Signed_____

Dated _____

Address _____

1ˢᵗ Aspect -- LOVABLE

The first and most important aspect of love is that of being *lovable*. There must be love from self to self before it can be extended to others. You cannot give from an empty cup. Fill your cup of divine self-love to overflowing. You are lovable in spite of any shortcomings and faults. Learn to love your individuality and your connection with God.

2ᴺᴰ Aspect -- LOVING

The second aspect of love is that of *loving*, whereby you give and express love to others and self. Loving others comes naturally and easily when you fully love yourself.

3ʳᵈ Aspect -- LOVED

The third aspect of love is that of *being loved*. You need to allow yourself to be loved and to fully receive love from others. When you strive daily to achieve these three states, you will come to understand the true meaning of unconditional love. To achieve unconditional love in your life, all three of these aspects must be happening simultaneously.

Everyone needs love—no matter how independent, wealthy, or successful a person may be. Without love, there is no self-actualization. Love is an element as essential to our well-being as air or water.

Love Magic Magnetic Carpet

Stand in front of the window and with your arms outstretched from your sides turn slowly from left to right (clockwise) saying the following Affirmation--

"I, (your name) now magnetize from the sun, moon, stars and entire solar system, peace, anticipation, faith, love and my special Love Partner right here and right now, for which I give thanks!"

You will be saying this sentence as you perform the Magic Magnetic Circle Exercise.

Remember this is your Order to the Universe. If you give a confused order, you may receive a confused answer or manifestation. Use the following Sample Master Affirmation adding your own wishes and desires. Feel free to change this Sample Affirmation, delete, add to it, etc. Make it yours. The words that come from deep within you are the words that add power to all Affirmations.

Be sure that you do not order up a certain person. If you like the looks of a person, you can put that picture on your table with the words, "Someone that looks like him or her." I would suggest you select a drawing, photo, etc of a person with a great smile and loving eyes.

Just a sketch of that person is fine. You must not affirm and magnetize a certain person to you, unless you are in a relationship with him or her and wish to make it more loving. The other person must desire the same result.

Everyone has free choice and that person has to want to be with you. All Affirmations and magnetizing must have the safety clause incorporated into it. The safety clause is, we affirm everything and everyone to the good of all parties concerned--and that includes you!

The Affirmation Process is so powerful that it comes with a warning and what I call—

Sample Master Affirmation for Love

Picture or sketch of the person you desire

"I, (your name), deserve and now have and enjoy a loving, lasting, happy relationship (which turns into marriage, if that is what you desire) with the perfect man/woman for me. This person is unattached, kind, loving, generous, nice-looking, healthy mentally and physically and emotionally, balanced, faithful, financially independent, and on a similar spiritual path. (Add whatever you wish here). He/she accepts and loves my family as I accept and love his/her family. We enjoy walking, bowling, skiing, biking, etc. (Fill in what activities you wish.) He/she loves and adores me as I love and adore him/her. This person accepts me just the way I am and I accept him or her just the way he/she is. We encourage and help each other to grow, evolve and become the very best we can be. We are happy to the good of all parties concerned. Thank you, thank you, thank you.

I fully accept"

Signed _____

Dated _____

Address _____

When you date and sign this Master Affirmation, you have made a firm and binding contract with your higher self, God, Universal Mind or whomever you believe in.

Relationship Puzzle

Attracting that special relationship is similar to putting a jigsaw puzzle together. Challenges are only pieces of the larger puzzle. You may need to find solutions to each part of it. Even the smallest piece of the puzzle is important and, if it is missing, the whole puzzle is incomplete. When you are working on solving the whole puzzle, this often involves other people and situations.

All relationships require work, trust, loving kindness, and consideration. How much energy and loving kindness are you prepared to put into your relationship-finding? How important is your puzzle? Put your very own relationship puzzle together piece by wonderful piece today. Problems are only pieces of the larger puzzle and you may need to find the solution to each part.

It is important to keep in mind that you must never force a person to commit to you. It has to be his or her decision. It is also important to get agreement from each party before fitting that piece into the main part of the puzzle. That other person must want a relationship with you as much as you do.

When involved in the *Relationship Puzzle* you are always searching for the right pieces. Carefully examine each one. Perhaps it contains a lesson you need to learn. Can you see that a loving *Relationship Puzzle* cannot contain seeds of dishonesty, mistrust and betrayal? Even if a piece looks to you as if it will fit perfectly, when you place it next to the other piece you may discover that it does not.

If this happens, it is time to take a look at yourself and discover exactly what you desire. If it is a small piece (e.g. a little anger or resentment) and you think you can ignore it or leave it out, think again, as your puzzle will never be complete without *all* the pieces. As you pick up each piece, gaze at it intently and ask for any guidance or input.

Then ask if there are any lessons or information that you need to know in order to proceed. If the answer is yes, sit quietly and listen. In the case of the 'fear of commitment piece,' of the Relationship Puzzle, you may have the puzzle shaping up just great, but when it comes time to place that piece, you cannot get it to fit. Then it is time to go within and do some soul-searching.

Ask if it is time to forgive, dissolve and release any blocks from previous relationships. Also ask yourself what it is that you really desire. You may need to curb your possessive ways or streak of jealousy. Or it could be that the person (piece) that you are trying so desperately to fit into the puzzle, may not be the right person for you at all! Go within and ask yourself. Your inner guide or Higher Self is the superglue that holds the pieces of the inner you in place.

You will learn about the various types of people and you may choose to use particular pieces of the puzzle that you apply to your prospective mate. Mark the pieces, *healthy, happy, independent, kind, balanced, loving, generous, faithful, kind, caring, financially independent, nice appearance* and more. When you put all the pieces together you may discover that the person you are doing it for is the right person for you, but needs a few minor adjustments.

We can never change others, but we can change this way in which we view them and most often they sense the change in you and they respond accordingly. Ask yourself how much you are willing to compromise. Then do a Relationship Puzzle for yourself and find out what kind of mate you are, or will be. You may also discover some values or desirable qualities are missing. You can then develop them by embarking on the *Personal Contract Affirmation Process.*

Relationship Train

Your train of life– Who is getting on and off your train?

This is a way of letting go of old and negative relationships that are not working for you. Perhaps that person or persons have learned all they can from their relationship with you and need to experience another relationship. This may be true for you as well.

I believe you were given your train of life when you were born into this world. Then as you grew older, it was your decision whether or not to keep certain people on your train. Sometimes they wanted to disembark and other times they were content to stay put. I use the Relationship Train as an analogy to describe the various parts of relationships.

As you read and study the Relationship Train, really think about yourself. Which car are you presently on? Are you happy there? If you are not, then you can change it as you desire. You are the 'engineer' of your own train.

The Relationship Train is always on track, on time and dependable. To attract that perfect, lasting, loving relationship, you have to be in the marketplace (to mix metaphors!). Boarding the Relationship Train is the process of placing yourself in the marketplace. You are never turned away. All are welcomed equally. The Relationship

Train is like a passenger train with many cars, and everyone boards and disembarks at will. You are free to move throughout the train at any time. The conductor is your subconscious mind or Higher Self that guides and protects you along the way.

The Engine

This is the place where all relationships begin. You are in a relationship with yourself at birth. You are always in some form of relationship, whether negative or positive. The physical part of all relationships is created in the engine and is fueled by the emotions of desire and passion. The engine is the first car. It could be called *The Creation Car*.

The Sleeping Car

This is the comfort zone car. Your porters are fear and phobias and they are at your beck and call. They provide you with clean bedding (excuses), comfortable surroundings (more excuses, blame, judgment, and other explanations) that keep you in your comfort zone. Your comfortable surrounding is the process of blaming others for your misfortunes and never taking responsibility for your own actions. This could also be the sulking or silent area where one partner goes to sulk. This is his or her secret room, car or hiding spot in the mind. This is *The Sulking Car* or *Stuck Car*.

The Dining Room Car

This car is a place to talk, communicate and resolve issues. This is a fully functioning car that leads to growth, happiness, long, lasting, loving relationships and marriages. Stay here as long as you desire. Some people find loving, happy relationships or marriages and stay in this car for their entire lifetimes. This is *The Fully Functioning Car*.

The Club Car

This car is for socializing, enjoying, relaxing, meeting other singles and communicating on a fun level. No long-term commitments are made here. It could be called *The Hang Loose Car*.

The Baggage Car

This is where all personal baggage is placed. You can leave it there to be disposed of, or you may take it with you. The choice is yours. It may be the time to get rid of any unwanted, negative baggage. When leaving this car, be careful not to pick up another person's baggage. You may find it heavier or more troublesome than your own. This is *The Disposing of Baggage Car*.

The Caboose

This is the last car of the *Relationship Train*. It is the place of ending relationships. People who want to end relationships enter and visit this car. This is a place of endings and brand new beginnings and is also known as *The Ending One Relationship and Beginning Another Relationship Car*.

There are various boarding stations (choices, ways and paths) all along the way. People board these cars at will and they stay as long as they wish. They can get off whenever they choose. This is a train of free choice. Are you on the *Relationship Train?* What car will you stop at and for how long? Every day men and women are deciding which train to board, then which car to retreat to in every relationship. At any time you can visit the other cars or feel free to get off that particular *Relationship Train* and board another train. This process is ongoing and you will always be boarding, staying or getting off the train. It delivers everyone who chooses to board it, to his or her destination of choice.

Choose your particular train and retreat to the car of your choosing. If your partner desires and chooses to get off your *Relationship Train,* allow him or her to do so. Release them with loving kindness to their highest good. When one relationship is finished and the grieving process is completed, you are ready for another relationship opportunity to appear. This can apply to any friendship or relationship.

Affirmation Light Bulb for Relationship/Marriage

Invite your partner to participate in this exercise, making a private space together. This can be very romantic, exciting, and fulfilling. One couple who made their own mental Marriage Affirmation Light Bulb swears it saved their marriage. They used it as a safe and sacred place in which to settle disagreements, make love, and talk openly about their feelings. They had a place to run away to, even if it was only in their minds. The whole procedure was very real to them. They incorporated creative visualization, imagination, and reality. Now that they are in a better financial position, they do the same exercise on the physical plane, joking that their expensive hotel room is their very own mental Marriage Affirmation Light Bulb.

Sample Master Affirmation for Happy Relationships

"I (your name), deserve and NOW have happy, healthy and harmonious relationships with my family, co-workers, employers and everyone that I come into contact with. I know the most important relationship I will ever have is the one I have with myself. I am full of loving kindness and happy to the good of all parties concerned. Thank you, thank you, thank you.

I fully accept"

Signed _____

Dated _____

Address _____

Affirmations When Properly Done Always Work!

RETIREMENT AFFIRMATION TOOLS

Putting Your Ideas and Business Techniques into a Pink Balloon

Place all your ideas and business success secrets into a pink balloon and release it into the Universe to be accessed by anyone just starting out in a new career or anyone in need of help.

Your Retirement Career

Retirement can be wonderful. Far from being the end of life, it can bring freedom from all the obligations and schedules that restricted and determined your life in the past. It can, therefore, be a time of great personal fulfillment. The secret to a happy, full retirement is to find something to do that you love. You can leave all the *should haves* behind and start on the *dreams* of life.

A New Beginning: Scary or Exciting?

You have given many prime years of your life to your family, career, and making money to live. Now it is time for *you* to pursue your interests and fondest, wildest dreams. Instead of viewing retirement as the *golden handshake* or the end of your life, look at it as the exciting, fun-filled opportunity for you to do what you desire. Retirement does not mean giving up, or the end of life. It heralds a whole new beginning.

It is time to enjoy the rewards of your life's work and harvest the seeds you have sown. Make the latter part of your life exciting and wonderful so that you look forward to every day with enthusiasm, joy, and anticipation.

Sit Down in a Quiet Place and Really Think About Your Retirement

There are two possible ways to approach retirement. You may experience excitement when you retire, knowing you are now free to do all the things you never had time to do and pursue what really interests you. Or you may be devastated and paralyzed by fear of the unknown, thinking, "What will I do? My life is finished. There is no reason to live. No one needs me. I am useless without my career."

Those in the second category have lost their professional identities and are like the 'walking dead.' They have given up on their dreams and, without goals or plans, are merely existing.

They have lost their zest for living. Negative, habitual thinking has hypnotized them and they do not know what it is like to really live. They are just waiting to physically die and be buried and forgotten.

Which approach would you choose?

Life is to be lived and enjoyed, not just endured. Assuming that you have budgeted and planned for this time of your life and are financially secure, it is time to enjoy. For those of you less fortunate, it may be necessary to find other types of part-time work to supplement your income. If that is the case, start the Personal Contract Affirmation Method immediately, affirming for that perfect, successful, part-time, lasting career or small business for you.

Write down the 'Two Ways to Approach Retirement.' Make two columns, one for negative and one for positive. In one column, write down all the negative things about retiring, and in the other column, list all the advantages to retiring, like having time to do what you really love to do.

Moving Out of Your Comfort Zone

My Experience When I Retired from Real Estate

I retired from the real estate profession after more than twenty years. When butterflies started flying around in my stomach, I said, "Stop. Listen up, self. I have worked all my life. I am entitled to some relaxation and enjoyment. I give myself permission to do whatever I choose."

When I retired, I visualized placing all the ideas, experiences, business and marketing plans and expertise I had ever used during my business lifetime in a soft, pink cloud. As I visualized it floating up into the blue sky, I said, "I now release every part of this information with loving kindness. I release it to create substance for anyone who wishes to use it to benefit or to further his or her business, career, life, and growing process. I know that when good, positive, constructive ideas are lovingly released into the Universe, anyone may tap into that information and benefit accordingly."

During my business lifetime, I was a school secretary, waitress, restaurant owner, author, legal secretary, and promotion director and more. I was also a realtor, both in Canada and the United States. I am now Anne Marie—mother, author, lecturer, teacher, and friend. Sometimes we identify with what we do. Being too attached to that identity can make it difficult for us to find another purpose later in life.

If I say I am a realtor, I lose that identity when I retire or am no longer able to do my job. It is therefore better to say, "I am Anne Marie and I am in the real estate profession." This way, I am identifying with myself as a person, not a realtor. As Wayne Dyer says, "We are not what we do. If we are what we do, when we don't, we aren't."

Since my retirement from real estate, I have been very busy doing what I love to do—spending precious time with my family and friends, travelling, hosting my own Radio/Internet show; writing my Affirmation books; Articles and monthly newsletters; columns; counselling; teaching seminars; answering numerous e-mails; conducting workshops on the power of Affirmations, and much more. I also completed my ministerial studies. I make numerous guest appearances on radio and television shows. I thoroughly enjoy visiting, writing, meditating, walking, playing, laughing, reading, and travelling. I can also take advantage of doing absolutely nothing and having fun!

Make plans and look forward to excitement and joyous expectation to your retirement career!

Using the Inward, Outward and Action Parts

Retirement can be wonderful. Far from being the end of life, it can bring freedom from all the obligations and schedules that restricted and determined your life in the past. It can, therefore, be a time of great personal fulfillment. The secret to a happy, full retirement is to find something to do that you love. You can leave all the *should haves* behind and start on the *dreams* of life.

Retirement is just as much a career or livelihood as were your working years. The good news is now you can manage your life the way you desire. This is the time of your life that you can exercise your power as manager, supervisor, and boss over yourself and your life.

You can get up when you want, schedule your appointments to your advantage, and live your day as you desire. To help you get the best out of your retirement career, you can divide it into three segments, as follows.

1. Inward Part

This is where you go *inward* to focus on loving, respecting, and approving of yourself. Breathe in love, peace, and joy; breathe out worry, fear, or frustration. Find out who you are, why you are here, and where you wish to go. Take long, luxurious baths and meditate, relax, and enjoy the simple things of life.

Get in touch with self and nature

SEE	the creations of God all around
HEAR	the wind blowing through the trees
FEEL	its soft, gentle breeze on your face
SMELL	that beautiful rose
TASTE	a wild strawberry or chew on a blade of grass

Discover your passion in life, become involved with others, and follow your dream. As I always say, "Fall in love with what you do and you never have to work again." I believe and live this!

2. *Outward Part*

This aspect of your retirement career involves projecting your good energy out into the Universe and to others. Extend your hand in help and love to those who need it. Visit the lonely and wipe away the tears of the brokenhearted. Share yourself and your talents with others. Give the gift of yourself to a loved one in a healthy sexual relationship.

Give back to the community and the Universe. Nurture old friendships and create new ones. Teach, help, and share with family members and friends. Become involved in charity work, church activities, or fund-raising ventures. Create and develop ideas of your own. Start your own home-based business doing what really interests you!

Many senior citizens have become multimillionaires in their 70s, 80s, and even 90s. You are in control. Make it your intention to enjoy this part of your life and do it! And, most important, have *fun!*

3. *Action Part*

This part involves taking action and seizing every day as precious and filled with exciting opportunities. Do all the things you once only dreamed of doing. Take a trip to somewhere you have always dreamed of visiting. Create a hobby or become that famous artist, writer, or musician.

Do physical things, such as bowling, golfing, knitting, or whatever you desire. Study, read the *Bible*, self-improvement books, articles, and listen to uplifting shows on television. Keep yourself informed of new experiments and products.

Exercise to improve your health. If you have some health concern, find out all you can about it. If you suffer from pain, find ways to lessen, manage, or get rid of it. Fill your mind with positive thoughts, ideas, and concepts.

Get out and make your dreams come true. This could be the time to share with the world your invention, new book, song, poem, or tape. There are no deadlines being imposed by others. *You* make the deadlines in your retirement career. You can stay up late at night and *sleep in*, if you desire.

Talk about interesting subjects and positive, happy things; people will love to be in your company. Drop the 'me, me' talk and be truly interested in the other person and talk about his or her interests.

If you are widowed, lonely, or desire companionship in your life, get busy and meet that special person. Some people prefer to lead the single life; others prefer to be married. This is a matter of personal choice. If you wish to attract that special person into your life, follow the instructions in this book for attracting the perfect partner for you.

You may desire the company of a part-time companion to attend shows, have dinner, travel, go on long walks, or have chats by the fireside. You have learned how thoughts and the mind can change your life for the positive and give you control over your situations. Decide what you want to have happen in your life and make it happen!

Some individuals spend years grieving for a deceased spouse or partner, not realizing they have numerous other opportunities for happiness with other partners. Rather than getting stuck in the past, they could pursue new interests and allow other lonely, single people to have the gift of their companionship.

Find and live your bliss. By doing this, you are giving others permission to do the same. This can be the most exciting time of your life. It is a time for fresh, new beginnings and a time for rejoicing. Become involved 100 %. Plan something exciting. Take up a hobby you thoroughly enjoy. Make it one that will help others. Become completely involved. This is your life. Live it to the fullest!

Become Younger, Using Your Mind

Give up all thoughts of ageing. Age can be used as an excuse for not doing certain things. Affirm that your lifespan is in excess of 120+ healthy, active, happy, prosperous years. Intention is a very powerful force. Say often, "It is my intention to grow younger and I do!"

Holding grudges and being unforgiving of self and others can age you far beyond your years. It can also lead to depression, anxiety, and wrinkles, robbing you of your happiness.

Love and respect your body. Meditate and learn to control the stress level in your life. Spend time complimenting and approving of every part of your body. Affirm that every cell, tissue, organ, bone, and every part of your body is now regenerating, rejuvenating, energizing, and becoming younger and younger. When you exercise, repeat over and over, "Younger and younger. I am becoming younger and younger." Do not buy into the old-age mentality. Watch your self-talk.

Refrain from saying, "I'm too old," or "I haven't got many years left, I can't do that at my age." Instead say, "I am growing younger and becoming slimmer and healthier every day. Time stands still for me. I have all the time in the world. Time is my friend. I enjoy and now live a long, healthy, happy life, in excess of 120 years."

Reserve now for your 120+ birthday party. Visualize yourself healthy, young-looking, and supple. See your family and friends enjoying the occasion with you and — oh, yes — have fun!

Laugh and have fun. Laughter is one of the best medicines. Laughing and having fun is an important part of my life. I laugh and have fun every day!

Your Choice

Remember, it is all up to you and you alone to determine your degree of happiness. Every person is different; what is right for you may not be right for another. You make the choice and the Laws of the Universe will support whichever path you choose.

Thank the Creator for this wonderful day and for your creative power. You can carve out peace, joy, and happiness for yourself and others.

Sample Master Affirmation for a Happy Retirement

"I, (your name), deserve to have and now enjoy a rewarding, happy retirement. I keep busy doing what I want to do. I am safe. I give myself permission to enjoy my retirement. I am fulfilled, happy, and involved. I am now free to pursue all my unfulfilled dreams. I enjoy time spent with loved ones. I believe in my future.

I now do things I only dreamed of doing. I enjoy travelling, fishing, golfing, walking on the beach, and just relaxing.

I believe in myself and my choices. I choose to be and am healthy, involved in life, and peaceful. I choose to and think positive, uplifting thoughts. I enjoy caring and sharing. I am happy, to the good of all parties concerned. Thank you, thank you, thank you.

I fully accept"

Signed_____

Dated _____

Address _____

Affirmations When Properly Done Always Work!

SELF-ESTEEM AFFIRMATION TOOLS

Act 'As If'

Act as if you are feeling wonderful about yourself and that you are exactly as you wish to be. Remember the song, 'Whistle a happy tune and no one will know you are afraid?'

Let's use this one for loving, respecting and approving of yourself. When you hold the feelings and emotions of self-approval and healthy self-love, it becomes a habit and creates grooves in your subconscious mind to anchor those wonderful feelings. And through the Law of Attraction, these types of good, healthy, positive thoughts attract more of the same!

Anchor Good Feelings

Go back into your past, gently close your eyes and remember and bring to the front burner of your mind a memory of a time when you felt absolutely wonderful and everything was going well for you. As you remember this feeling, gently but firmly anchor that feeling to your heart area. Really feel it with every fiber of your being in your heart chakra. Then open your eyes, saying, "Thank you, thank you, thank you."

My Experience in Anchoring

When I was feeling down and experiencing thoughts of low self-esteem, I found a comfortable place to sit; I closed my eyes, counted backwards from number 9 to number 1 to help me relax further. Then I searched my mind for a picture of me when I felt good about myself.

When I located that image and situation, I experienced it in my mind in complete detail. I was the main speaker for a group of over 200 women and I felt in control. I saw exactly what I was wearing, how my hair was done, how I was standing and what I was saying. Then I heard the standing ovation that I received at the end of my talk and I could feel my self-esteem starting to soar. I sat there for a few moments, feeling that wonderful successful feeling and then I brought that memory together with its wonderful, positive emotion and feelings into the present. I filed it neatly in my memory bank so I can go back whenever I wish and re-experience it. Try it and see what happens for you.

Block of Ice

Visualize your body as a huge block of ice. Imagine chopping and chiselling away at it until you uncover *the real you* hidden deep inside. Focus on forgiving and releasing all negativity, cutting away all that is not really you. Feel the power of discernment fill your body as you imagine yourself being able to say "No," whenever necessary.

As the layers of self-doubt, criticism, and all forms of negative thoughts and feelings about self are chopped away, a beautiful image emerges.

You are special. There is no one else exactly like you. Your heart, mind, and body are filled with self-confidence, self-worth, and love. Your ice carving is complete and you are whole. See this image vividly in your mind and keep concentrating and focusing on it. Think it into existence.

Love, respect, and approve of yourself, just the way you are.

In the media, we hear increasingly about alternative healing methods used in the treatment of illness and disease. Doctors cannot explain the cures. One woman, for example, was diagnosed with cancer which she was told would require surgery. She visualized her tumour as a huge block of ice inside her body. Then she visualized taking a kettle of boiling water and pouring it over the block of ice every day (just like defrosting the refrigerator).

After several weeks of this concentrated visualization, the block of ice had completely melted in her mind's eye. When she visited her doctor, he reported that the cancerous tumour had miraculously disappeared and that there was no need to operate. Just as negative thoughts can have powerful impacts on our bodies, so, too, can positive, healing thoughts.

3 Important Aspects of Love

Write three columns titled Lovable, Loving and Loved. Now write under each column three ways you feel you are lovable, then write three ways you feel that you are loving and complete by writing three ways you feel you are loved.

Ask the Following Questions:

- » Are you satisfied with what you have written?
- » Do you wish to add to any of the columns? If so, do it!
- » Really think about what you have added
- » Can you really feel that love saturating every cell of your body?
- » How does it feel for you?

When you feel the exercise is complete, say, "Thank you, thank you, thank you." And go on with your day.

Remember to read what you have written in this exercise often. This simple, yet powerful exercise provides a great deal of clarity as you uncover and discover things about YOU!

How can we expect others to love us unless we love ourselves? We cannot give from an empty cup. You need to have a healthy love of self before you can expect others to love you. It is vital to have your cup of love filled to overflowing so it will overflow to others.

Let's Talk again about the importance of L O V E

1st Aspect -- LOVABLE

The 1st and most important aspect of love is that of being *lovable*. There must be love from self to self before it can be extended to others. You cannot give from an empty cup. Fill your cup of divine self-love to overflowing. You are lovable in spite of any shortcomings and faults. Learn to love your individuality and your connection with God.

2nd Aspect -- LOVING

The 2nd aspect of love is that of loving, whereby you give and express love to others and self. Loving others comes naturally and easily when you fully love yourself.

3rd Aspect -- LOVED

The 3rd aspect of love is that of *being loved*. You need to allow yourself to be loved and to fully receive love from others.

When you strive daily to achieve these three states, you will come to understand the true meaning of unconditional love. To achieve unconditional love in your life, all three of these aspects must be happening simultaneously.

Everyone needs love—no matter how independent, wealthy, or successful a person may be. Without love, there is no self-actualization. Love is an element as essential to our well-being as air or water.

Mirror

Look into the mirror every morning and evening and say to the person looking back at you, "Hey, you are beautiful (or handsome). You are awesome and totally wonderful. You look so radiantly healthy."

Note: Self-talk is very important. The way you speak to yourself about yourself determines your life. Past negative thoughts have created your reality today and now you can create a new reality by replacing that negativity with positive, happy self-talk. Your subconscious mind is your humble servant, bringing to you, through the Law of Attraction, exactly what you desire. It believes everything you say.

So to recap, if you say, "I am broke," your subconscious mind will keep you broke. Your car gives up the ghost, your washing machine breaks down or your computer crashes. Your subconscious mind simply does the job of manifesting whatever it is programmed to bring forth. As you change your thoughts and mind, you change your life accordingly.

Stepping Outside Your Comfort Zone

Simply make a decision to take control of your life, step out of the 'norm' for you, and stretch your imagination. Sit and visualize in your mind what it would be like to do, be, have whatever you desire.

Create a vivid picture in color of that event. Bring in your five physical senses.

SEE	yourself being in the limelight
HEAR	people saying, "(Your name), I am so impressed with you (whatever you are doing)"
SMELL	your favorite scent
FEEL	how absolutely wonderful you feel
TASTE	either a drink of fresh, sparkling water or visualize biting into a juicy apple to complete the 5 physical senses

This way you are transporting yourself from the present into the wonderful future that you desire. Remember that the process of doing Affirmations properly is the bridge that connects the present to the future and future events.

Step Process to Increase Self-Love

One of my clients, Roy, came to me with the following problem. He said he did not love himself -- in fact, he said he actually loathed himself. He said it was impossible to go from loathing himself to loving himself. I suggested he do the Step Process. I also suggested that he take his time with each step and that he stay on each step until he really felt that way.

He did and he was able to come to a place of self-love one step at a time. Roy's starting place was the feeling of "I loathe myself."

Step Process

Step 1 I tolerate myself

Step 2 I accept myself

Step 3 I respect myself

Step 4 I approve of myself

Step 5 I like myself;

Step 6 I love myself.

Increasing Your Self-Love

Sit down in a quiet place, close your eyes gently and think about YOU.

How do you really feel about yourself? Are you angry at some person or event, past or present? Do you feel that you are not good enough? Or that you can't do whatever you wish to do?

Talk to Your Body Parts - Healthy Hair

Select an area of your body that you wish to improve upon.

For Example

You wish to have healthy, shining, thick hair on your head area — Say, "I deserve and now have healthy, thick, shiny hair." Then in the morning, rub your head to get the circulation going and gently but firmly pull your hair. Do this exercise with love and gratefulness. Then say, "Thank you, thank you, thank you," and go on about your day.

Toothbrush Exercise

Increase Healthy Self-Love

When you brush your teeth, or just after, look into the mirror at yourself and say, "Hey self you are a great person. I now forgive everyone and everything that has ever hurt me. I NOW forgive MYSELF. I start this moment loving, respecting and approving of ME!"

Step 1   This is where your feelings of self reside. For example you could be angry for not speaking up for yourself

Step 2   Lighten up on yourself. Tell yourself that you too, are human

Step 3   Start counting and accepting the good and positive things about you and what you do

Step 4   Beginning to appreciate and like yourself

Step 5 - Start the feelings of love, appreciation, respect & approval for self welling up in you

S M I L E – My own interpretation of the word SMILE

S   Simple

M   Message

I   I

L   Love

E   Everyone

It costs nothing – gives much! It also brings out your inner beauty and youthfulness. Never underestimate the power of a genuine and loving smile! You could give another person joy without evening knowing by smiling at them. It could be the only recognition they have experienced that day.

This Too Shall Pass

This is a very important and helpful exercise. I use it often and rely on it as one of my wonderful Affirmation Tools.

When I am in an uncomfortable and/or negative situation, I simply visualize on the back of my ring these four words, "This too shall pass," and it does, together with the good times. This is what we call life. I really see in my mind's eye these 4 words and receive power and comfort from them.

Sample Master Affirmation for Self-Esteem

"I, (your name), deserve and now have and enjoy good, healthy self-esteem. I love, respect and approve of myself and my life, who I am, what I am doing and who I am associating with. I love being healthy, loving and peaceful to the good of all parties concerned. Thank you, thank you, thank you.

I fully accept"

Signed _____

Dated _____

Address _____

Affirmations When Properly Done Always Work!

215

SPIRITUAL GROWTH AFFIRMATION TOOLS

Divine Wisdom and Divine Order

I use this Divine Order Tool often, whenever a negative situation occurs that needs straightening out, such as a disagreement, or any situation that needs clearing. I also use both Divine Wisdom and Divine Order in work situations and in our Nightly Affirmation Group Prayer.

Divine Order

Write 'Divine Order' with a felt pen on a small piece of paper and place it on your telephone. When I do this, I am amazed at how my phone messages change. Only the people I wish to speak with call and, when they do, we have a wonderful conversation.

My Experience with Divine Order on Telephone

When my telephone rings excessively with nuisance calls, I take a felt pen and write on masking tape these two words, 'Divine Order.' I then put it right on my telephone. I was totally amazed at the startling results. Yes, I still did receive ALL my important and welcome calls, but gone were the nuisance ones.

One of my readers works at a company in their refund or complaint department. All day, he deals with irate and unhappy customers. He wrote two letters on a piece of masking tape – 'D.O.' which is short for Divine Order and placed it on his phone. He was reluctant to put the words as that could create some challenges. He reported back that his customers now still complain, but they do not do it in the abusive way they did before he did this exercise. Of course, in his mind before he picks up the phone, he whispers to himself, "Divine Order" over and over. He is a strong believer and says this short exercise helped him stay in that position for the amount of time needed so he could attend University.

Lighthouse

I use this method when I hear of an earthquake or other disaster at home and in various parts of the world. I visualize a brilliant, bright, clear light shining out into the ethers and atmosphere to give people hope and strength to go on. In that beam of God's brilliant, pure light, I place thoughts of love, healing, hope and prosperity for anyone to tune into.

Have you ever been in a lighthouse? When I visited one, I was amazed at how many magnifications that light went through to make it brilliant, bright, and clear, and to shine out into the water to help guide captains and people safely to shore. I thought to myself that no matter how strong the storm was, how high the waves, how much lightning and thunder was going on around that beam of light, nothing could touch it as it kept on doing its job shining brightly--a port in the time of storm. If I was connected to God's wonderful power and light like that beam, it would not matter what was going on around me--I would be bright, clear and steadfast.

Find a quiet place to sit. Clear your mind of negative and unnecessary thoughts. Visualize yourself in a lighthouse building. See all various types of lights, the magnifying equipment and things necessary to run a lighthouse operation. See yourself connecting with that wondrous light that is going out into the atmosphere. Visualize yourself being connected to God's powerful light. Say, "No matter how bad the storm or what happens, my connected light is not affected. The wind can blow; the seas rage; and lightning strike, but my light is not affected because it is of a different frequency. Now you are in a position to send that White Light of God out into the world." When you feel you are complete, then say "Thank you, thank you, thank you," and go on with your day.

Nightly Affirmation – Group Prayer
Join in with our---

Nightly Affirmation/Prayer--
"Dear Father, God/Creator, Universal Mind, Higher Self, or whomever you believe in--

Thank you for all our blessings and even for those who don't seem like blessings, and we accept and learn from the lessons therein. We jointly and severally affirm for Divine Wisdom and Divine Order to our World Leaders; Peace in the World; Healing, Love and Respect for Mother Earth; cure for cancer, aids and ALL disease; Healing and Protection to our Men and Women in the armed forces both here and overseas. Healing and Love for all those who are starving and suffering from world catastrophes.

We place a White Light--Dome of Protection over every one of our Affirmation/Prayer partners and their families and my family and me from the roots of our hair to the tips of our toes, all day today and every day all night today and every night and over everyone and everything around us.

We are all fully protected. Then we add our own personal prayer requests. We end the Affirmation Prayer with, "We now join in with any person, anywhere in the world, who is at this moment thinking thoughts of peace, joy and happiness and we jointly and severally send these thoughts into every corner of the world. This we ask in Your Name, Thank you, thank you, thank you." And so it is!

Serenity Prayer

God grant me the serenity
To accept the things I cannot change
The courage to change the things I can
And the wisdom to know the difference

Spiritual Disinfectant

On a piece of masking tape, write the words 'Spiritual Disinfectant.' Place the tape on a small spray bottle. Fill the bottle with water and, if you wish, add a drop or two of your favourite essential oil or perfume. When you encounter a negative situation, simply spray the air with the spray bottle, saying, "I now spray all negative thoughts and situations." You can also use this technique to spray away the negative thoughts of others, and even your own negative thoughts. (Note: Never spray a person in the face!)

Sometimes I use my Spiritual Disinfectant to spray my home before I have workshops or after a particularly negative person or persons have been visiting. Then I also spray with my Spiritual Disinfectant after the workshop to dissolve any negativity. I also use the Spiritual Disinfectant Tool in my mind. This is great, as I can do this silently and so no one notices. I believe it works as well as doing it physically because your subconscious mind does not know the difference between a real event and an imagined event.

Sample Master Affirmation for Spiritual Awareness

"I, (your name), now open up to and deserve higher levels of awareness. I am safe. I now meditate on all that is good, kind, and peaceful. All negativity and fear leave my body now. I attract peace, goodness, and harmony. My mind is free from worry because I am in direct contact with the source of God's power and intelligence. This enables me to dissolve the cause of worry. I am calm and handle any situation. I am free of fear and worry. I believe in myself and my life. I experience new levels of spirituality, tranquility, love, peace, and joy. I am happy, to the good of all parties concerned. Thank you, thank you, thank you.

I fully accept"

Signed_____

Dated _____

Address _____

Affirmations When Properly Done Always Work!

.

WEIGHT AFFIRMATION TOOLS

21 Day Agreement

When making agreements, Affirmations, listening to tapes, etc. we always encourage you to do it for a minimum of 21 days as studies have shown that it takes 21 days to make a habit. Make a 21-day agreement with yourself to abstain from sweets or any fattening food. Since it takes 21 days to develop a new habit, this exercise can be very powerful when practised in conjunction with your Affirmations.

If you miss a day doing the 21-day cycle, start again. Thank your body in advance for assisting you.

Agreement from Your Body

Ask for, and get, an agreement from the parts of yourself that say, "You could never drop weight," or "You are too fat." Often there is a part of us that is cynical about positive change. It is comfortable with the present condition and afraid to change. Talk to yourself and get all parts to agree that reducing your weight would be beneficial to all.

You may wish to affirm that all parts of your body are in agreement with your weight-reducing program and with your weighing your ideal weight. Give away your "fat person." clothes. Doing this creates a vacuum you can then fill with a new 'slim person' wardrobe.

Watch your caloric intake, exercise, drink eight to 10 glasses of water daily, and do your Affirmations faithfully.

And remember to love, respect, and approve of yourself, *just the way you are.* This acknowledgement gives you the power to change.

Block of Ice

Visualize your body as a huge block of ice. Imagine chopping and chiselling away at it until you uncover *the real you* hidden deep inside. Focus on forgiving and releasing all negativity, cutting away all that is not really you.

As the layers of self-doubt, criticism, and all forms of negative thoughts and feelings about self and your weight are chopped away, a beautiful, healthy, slim image emerges.

You are special. There is no one else exactly like you. Your heart, mind, and body are filled with self-confidence, self-worth, and love. Your ice carving is complete and you are whole. Your body is becoming slimmer and slimmer until you reach your desired weight and you are becoming firmer and firmer. See this image of the slim, healthy, vibrant, you vividly in your mind and keep concentrating and focusing on it. Think it into existence. Love, respect, and approve of yourself, just the way you are. Enjoy your slim, beautiful, firm and youthful body.

Bless Your Food

Before breakfast, lunch, dinner and any time you eat, bless your food and ask it to go to the right places in your body. Stop for 10 seconds and say quietly to yourself, "A few seconds in my mouth: a few minutes in my mouth; a few hours in my stomach and a lifetime on my hips."

Borrow Back – Create Vivid Pictures in Color in Your Mind

Go back into your mind bank using the Clear, Search and Retrieve Affirmation Tool to a time when you were successful in dropping weight.

Create a special occasion that you attended where you were the main speaker (or main attraction) after your had dropped your specific weight and felt really good about yourself.

SEE	the dress, outfit you were wearing and how wonderfully it fit you and showed off your new figure
FEEL	the pride of accomplishment and how absolutely thrilled you are
SMELL	your favorite fragrance or flower scent
HEAR	people saying, "(Your name), you look absolutely awesome. How much weight did you drop? You look years younger"
Taste	a drink of fresh sparkling water or visualize biting into a juicy apple

Now transport this vivid image from the past into your present. Experience all the emotion that you felt that day or evening.

Use this Borrow Back Affirmation Tool into your present Affirmation program.

Butter Exercise

When you have successfully dropped a pound or two, take a pound or pounds of butter from the fridge and carry it around for a few minutes. When you have dropped 5 pounds take a 5 pound bag of sugar or flour and do the same thing. This gives you the feeling of what that dropping one, two or five pounds actually feels like in your body. Even a two or three-pound reduction in weight is significant and will definitely make an impression on your subconscious mind. Becoming aware and actually starting your weight reduction program are the keys to weight reduction and maintenance.

Cravings Overcome

When you crave sweets, paint or sketch a picture in vivid color of your favourite dessert. Imagine that you are eating that food. Engage your five senses to make a more real and lasting impression on your subconscious mind.

SEE   the delicious food
HEAR   yourself chewing it
FEEL   your stomach filling up
SMELL   the wonderful aroma
TASTE   the delightful flavours

Then mentally pick up a giant eraser and rub out the image. Take a deep breath, relax, release, and let go completely. Notice how satisfied you feel after eating this imaginary food. This visualization works powerfully to satiate any sweet cravings you may have. I do this process with cake, ice-cream and sweets regularly. It really does satisfy my craving for sweets. The more real, colorful, exciting, and fun you make it, the more powerfully it works.

Drop Not Lose!

When you are affirming never say 'lose weight' instead say, "Drop, release, melt, burn," etc. When you say *lose* your mind automatically wants to help you find it, and it does so and sometimes with several added pounds.

Love Your Excess Fat and Weight Away

Affirmation Tool

Love your excess fat and weight away. When you drop a few pounds, reward yourself with a luxurious bath, invigorating stroll, some quiet time, perfume, an article of clothing, etc. Put your arms around yourself and say, "Self, I love you, I respect you, I approve of you, just the way you are. You are terrific! Keep up the good work!"

The habit of overeating has been learned; it can be unlearned by the same process. Loneliness and boredom can lead to overeating, so keep your life involved, interesting, and exciting.

Develop and enjoy a loving, nurturing relationship with yourself (the most important person in your Universe) and you will never be lonely. Keep busy doing things that interest you. Help others. Volunteer your time or do whatever you need to do to move out of your 'safe, overweight comfort zone.'

When you truly love yourself, there is no need to build barriers of excess fat and weight to keep you safe from being hurt by others. You are safe with yourself. Start molding the kind of future and shape you want—today!

Letter to Personal Angel

To My Personal Angel

"I love you; I bless you and I thank you for assisting me in my weight-releasing program. I also thank you for adjusting my metabolism and my appetite. Thank you for healing my inner child, guiding me to eat nourishing food, fresh fruits and vegetables, and for giving me the strength to avoid sweets, and greasy, fattening, high-fat foods. Thank you for being with me always, loving, guiding, and encouraging me. I am healthy and happy, to the good of all parties concerned. Thank you, thank you, thank you. Love from (your name)."

Signed _____

Dated _____

Address _____

Next Time Exercise

The next time, I will do it differently — then do it! Make the next time start that very second.

You have the power and now you need to access it, harness it, and make it work for you. You must change your internal picture to match the ideal weight picture you are affirming. They must both agree to make the Affirmation work and the difference in your life. Focus all the power of your mind on this one picture. If you don't focus or concentrate on the picture of your desired weight and direct your mind-power, the image moves here and there and scatters its focus.

Create a detailed mental picture of looking and weighing your ideal weight. Make it colorful, bringing in all the five senses. Did you know diet foods can be exciting and interesting? Did you know exercise is fun and that while having fun, you are suppressing your appetite?

Paint Brush Exercise

Use the Paintbrush Exercise to Drop Weight

When you crave sweets, paint or sketch a picture in vivid color of your favourite dessert.

Imagine that you are eating that food. Engage your five senses to make a more real and lasting impression on your subconscious mind.

SEE   the delicious food
HEAR   yourself chewing it
FEEL   your stomach filling up
SMELL the wonderful aroma
TASTE   the delightful flavours

Then mentally pick up a giant eraser and rub out the image. Take a deep breath, relax, release, and let go completely. Notice how satisfied you feel after eating this imaginary food. This visualization works powerfully to satiate any sweet cravings you may have. I do it with butterscotch sundaes regularly. It really does satisfy my craving for sweets. The more real, colorful, exciting, and fun you make it, the more powerfully it works.

Signs to Encourage Yourself

Post signs of encouragement everywhere. For example, put a 'Weight Reduction in Progress' sign on your refrigerator to give you a positive jolt of good energy. You can also put a sign in your car, office, bedroom, and bathroom, declaring the ideal weight you wish to achieve. Make your Affirmations fun by singing, chanting, or shouting them out loud with lots of enthusiasm.

Refrain from putting *all* the emphasis on the numbers that appear on the scale. It took time to gain that extra weight, so it will naturally take time to remove it. Some weight-reduction programs suggest that you weigh yourself daily. I find once a week or even once a month to be more realistic when dropping weight. When maintaining your ideal weight, however, do weigh yourself daily.

Weight Flags Exercise

Another method you can use is to place 'red flags' on the fattening, rich food and gooey sweets. Allow your imagination to run wild and have fun with this process. You could even attach small signs. These could say, 'Dangerous to my health,' or 'Caution I could break out in bumps of fat.' Have fun developing your own, unique system.

Weight Lawn Mower Exercise

» First, she drinks a glass of water, then sits in a comfortable position and closes her eyes. She meditates for 10 minutes, putting herself in a state of creative visualization. She forgives herself and everyone and everything that has ever hurt her. She repeatedly tells her body that she loves, respects, and approves of it and that she is in control. She is aware of the fact that her thoughts affect her physical body.

» She orders her metabolism to speed up and visualizes it as a mini-lawnmower, shaving away her fat cells. She works on each area with her muscles flexed and her hands on that particular area at the same time. She then visualizes the fat cells melting away and sees her body as she would like it to look. (She claims there is scientific proof that when a person goes on a diet or starvation program, the body thinks it is starving and holds that memory in the fat cells.)

» She tells her body it is strong, efficient, and that it burns fat while she sleeps. She promises her body it will never be starved; therefore, there is no reason to hold onto all those reserve fat cells.

» She states she loves and craves fruit, vegetables, water, and exercise. She affirms she is strong, slim, beautiful, and smart. She visualizes the water she just drank washing away toxins and all the liquefied excess fat in her system. She emerges from her creative visualization exercise refreshed, feeling alive, healthy, and slim.

Sample Master Affirmation for Weight Releasing

"I, (your name), deserve and now weigh the ideal weight for me. I am healthy, strong, vibrant, slim and vibrant. All EXCESS weight and fat now drop from my body from the right places. I keep the excess fat and weight off my body. I am mindful of my caloric intake, and I drink 8-10 glasses of water daily, reduce stress and exercise regularly. I am happy, fulfilled, slim, healthy and youthful to the good of all parties concerned. Thank you, thank you, thank you.

I fully accept"

Signed_____

Dated _____

Address _____

Affirmations When Properly Done Always Work!

TESTIMONIALS OF
DR. ANNE MARIE EVERS

You may be asking yourself, "Do these Master Affirmations, Short Form Affirmation and Affirmation Tools Really Work?"

If so, please read the following—

SOME OF 'OWN' MY FAVORITE AFFIRMATION TOOL SUCCESSES

I personally used the Master Affirmations and Short Form Affirmations (Affirmation Tools), known as '*the* program' to create the following successes.

1. THE JAMES HARVEY STORY--James the Musician

James Harvey was a homeless young man living on the streets of Vancouver when he started reading a copy of my book, *Affirmations, Your Passport to Happiness* that someone had given him.

He memorized the Short-Form Affirmations at the back of the book. Because he is a musician, he put the words to music and listened to these positive Affirmations over and over. Whenever he needed positive energy, he would listen to this tape, first thing in the morning, at night before drifting off to sleep, and in the middle of the night, when he could not sleep or when he needed to hear some positive reinforcement.

Miracles began taking place in his life. He manifested a place to live with a wonderful 87-year-old gentleman Richard (Daddy) Babb and his daughter Marcia.

When James called me, he said, "Anne Marie, you will never believe my story." I replied, "Yes, I will." We met and he told me of these wonderful miracles—how he had received clothes, musical equipment, a computer, and many other useful things. He now has a job teaching pre-schoolers in Vancouver and is pursuing his musical career. He asked me how he could give back to the Universe for the blessings he received. I asked him if he thought he could put together a musical CD we could use for our Children's Anti-Violence Program,

"The Affirm and Learn Enhancement Program." This program has been taught for the past 5 years in a 3rd grade class in Washington State and in North Vancouver, British Columbia, with excellent results.

With the positive words that I suggested, James went to work and created the music and lyrics, putting together a positive, musical CD. It is children singing songs intermingled with Richard (Daddy) Babb's voice reading Affirmations from my book. Richard passed away in 2002, but his memory and voice will always be with us. The CD was played at his Memorial Service Reception.

Thousands of people have heard and just love this CD. They feel it helps children think positive thoughts and be kinder to one another. The CD was played for the 89th World Congress of the International New Thought Alliance in Phoenix, AZ, in 2003, and at the 90th INTA World Congress in Washington, DC, in 2004. It is also featured on a Radio/Internet Program broadcast that airs the last Monday of each month. This Radio/Internet Program reaches millions of people worldwide.

One day, James invited me to join him in teaching the Power of Affirmations at his school. The children really listened. I feel they learned so much about positive thoughts and how thoughts affect their daily lives. They also learned about The Ripple Effect (one of the songs featured on the CD), how to show kindness and pass it on to others, creating a positive ripple effect. James now has his own apartment and has taken this musical process a step further.

Such is the power of Affirmations when you access the power, harness the energy, and use it for positive outcomes. I am so proud of James and that his Affirmations are not only working in his life, he is influencing the next generation in a positive and uplifting way.

2. LINDA KOZINA – CREATING A FREE STANDING HOSPICE

For many years, the Crossroads Hospice Society held the vision of having our own free-standing hospice. After the land was selected, our task was to raise over $1,000,000 in capital funds.

We knew that Affirmations when properly done would produce results. From magazines, Dr. Anne Marie Evers and I fashioned a circle of pictures for our Hospice scrapbook, showing the desired colors and the home-like environment we wanted to achieve in the hospice. We wrote the names of the corporations, foundations, community leaders we wanted to contact and then added the positive words that would create the Magic

Magnetic Circle.

Over the course of four years, the Magic Circle enlarged. With the efforts of many dedicated community citizens and our Capital Campaign Chair Tracy Price, we were able to raise the funds to build our free-standing hospice. Thank you, Dr. Anne Marie. You were the catalyst that enabled us to fulfill our dreams. Linda Kozina, Hospice Manager, Crossroads Inlet Centre Hospice.

Magic Magnetic Circle
PROCEDURE

The Magic Magnetic Circle that Dr. Evers teaches is as follows---When you get up in the morning, clear your mind of any negative thoughts. Forgive everyone and everything that has ever hurt you, and then forgive yourself. Say, "I, (your name), now love, respect and approve of myself, just the way I am." Then add any person or group requests.

Following is the Magic Magnetic Circle Affirmation Tool that we used to create the free-standing Hospice.

Affirmation Success!

At our morning meetings, the four of us stood facing the window, slowly turning from left to right (clockwise) with our arms outstretched from our sides, saying the following Master Affirmation.

"We, (our names), now magnetize into our Magic Magnetic Circle (aura) peace, joy, love, health, happiness & money to our proposed Hospice, which extends to everyone we meet. We NOW joyfully and gratefully receive donations, grants, tithes and other monies from businesses, government agencies, individuals, etc to build a beautiful Hospice in Port Moody, BC Canada. This is built to the good of all parties concerned. We now see this

beautiful free-standing Hospice as complete, for which we say, "Thank you, thank you, thank you." We all fully accept on behalf of everyone.

Signed _____

Dated _____

_____

_____

We brought in the 5 physical senses when doing this Exercise.

SEE   We visualized in our minds in vivid color and detail the checks and money

HEAR   We heard people saying how happy they were to help us fund the Hospice to help so many people

SMELL   We had a favorite perfume and/or at times flowers

FEEL   We felt how happy we are to help create this wonderful Hospice

TASTE   We took a drink of fresh, sparkling water to complete the 5 Physical senses.

And it manifested as affirmed ! ! !

Then we said, "Thank you, thank you, thank you," and went on about our day.

As Dr. Evers teaches it is not selfish to magnetize these wonderful things to yourself first AND THEN extend them to every other person. You cannot give to others without first giving to yourself and you cannot give from an empty cup. You need to love and respect yourself before you can expect others to love and respect you.

3. THE PETER KIMBER STORY – From Despair to Triumph

Peter Kimber was Released From Prison in Mexico through the Power of Prayer and Affirmations!

It all started with a 'Prayer for Asking,' and ended with a 'Prayer of Thanksgiving!' I have always believed in the power of Affirmations, positive thinking and Prayer. I taught my children at a young age about the power of the spoken word --Affirmations and about the Law of Attraction which states what you think about you bring about; more gathers more; like attracts like; and what you are seeking is seeking you.

I always knew that as a Minister and Doctor of Divinity, I would be called upon to step up to the plate and do what I can to help others, but never did I ever expect to be instrumental to start the ball rolling to release of a man from a prison in Mexico!

On October 25th, 2006 it happened for me. A real miracle, one you read about in the news or dream of. I met Jessie and Julia at a Women's Show in Abbotsford, BC, Canada and they both told my sister, Darlene, and I that all they wanted was for their dad to come home. I felt such love and caring for these two lovely girls. I asked, "Where is your Dad?" They said, "He is in a jail in Mexico." I said, "Oh I am so sorry." Why is he in jail? They said he was charged with fraud that is 'building without a permit.' They told me how worried they were about him.

So I took one of my books that I was selling at the Show, *Affirmations Your Passport to Happiness* and had both Jessica and Julia sign it with love to their Dad. Then both my sister Darlene and I signed it as well. Right there in the booth we all put our hands on the book and did an Affirmation/ Prayer' that Peter would be released from jail and brought home to his family. Also I told the girls that I would add this request to my nightly Affirmation/Prayer Session at 11:00 p.m. Later I told an influential friend about Peter Kimber and of my meeting with Peter's daughters and he joined in with me every night in Prayer with our Group.

It is interesting to note that both he and I had never met Peter Kimber in person. At times we asked ourselves, "How can a man whom we've never met or seen become such an important and integral part of our lives?"

I spoke to Peter Kimber many times on the telephone in prison in Mexico. At this particular time the prison provided a special phone line for the prisoners to make calls to their family. Of course each prisoner was allowed a certain amount of telephone time.

Every night at 11:00 p.m. we would join in with our Affirmation/Prayer Group and affirm for healing, protection and the quick release of Peter Kimber.

Now I am happy and thankful that this Goal/ Affirmation/Prayer is accomplished and Peter Kimber was released from jail! I was so honored to be present when Peter arrived at the Abbotsford International Airport just

138 days after we started the Affirmation/Prayer process. I will never forget that picture of Peter embracing his family and friends at his arrival. It proves to me once again that the power of Affirmation/Prayer and Visualization always work when done to the good of all parties concerned. For those 138 days our group all visualized in vivid color Peter Kimber arriving at the Airport greeted by his loving family and we kept this image on the front burner of our minds every day until he actually arrived home! Such is the power of Creative Visualization.

And it is true that truly one person can make a difference one new, positive thought at a time, one action at a time and I realize now that none of this would have happened if I had not stepped out of my comfort zone and taken action, Affirmed and Prayed for his quick release.

Oh yes, they were low valleys and high mountain tops during our 4 months and 16 days journey and at times I wondered exactly what I got myself into. On all of my regular Radio Shows I asked for the help from my listeners and today my heart is full of gratitude for all the love, Prayers, Affirmations and support that they so freely and loving gave Peter. Many a time I called my friend Greg Norman, Radio Personality from Rhode Island to join me in affirming for Peter Kimber's quick release. I also enlisted the Prayers of many people, churches, groups and institutions.

So to everyone, on behalf of Peter, his family, friends, supporters and I--we wish to say that our hearts are full of gratitude and to the wonderful media people who stepped up to the plate and brought global attention to the crusade for Peter and his family.

Some of my friends advised me not to get involved but I thought if I as a Minster cannot put myself out to help another person, who ever will? I am so humbled and grateful that God chose me to start the whole journey from despair to joy and happiness, from darkness to light and to God I give the glory! I say, "Thank you, thank you, thank," from the bottom of my heart. And so it is.

4. AFFIRMING FOR MY 3rd HUSBAND

Do Affirmations really work? Yes, Affirmations DO WORK! *Sometimes they do not appear to work in our time-frame or as we think they should, but they always work!*

I believe that we all do Affirmations, whether or not we are aware of them. When you say, "I will never meet my soul mate or special love partner; I am meant to be alone; No one wants to date me, etc," you are in fact doing a form of negative Affirmations. And the Law of Attraction which is one of the natural laws of the great Universe is always turned on, (in fact you cannot turn it off), goes to work instantly to attract more of the same. As we have learned The Law of Attraction states that more gathers more, what you think about, you bring about, like attracts like and what you are seeking is seeking you.

MY PERSONAL MASTER AFFIRMATION

For That Lasting, Loving, Happy Relationship which turns into Marriage

I placed a picture of a man I like the looks of and I had no idea who this man was, nor do I wish to know. I wrote under that picture, 'that looks like him.' People are amazed when they see my Master Affirmation as Reg, my husband looks a great deal like the picture I put on my Master Affirmation.

(picture, sketch, etc.)

"I, Anne Marie Evers deserve and now have a lasting, loving, committed relationship which turns into marriage with the perfect man for me. (I know he will not be 'perfect' but he is perfect for me.) He is unattached, about 6', nice looking and healthy physically, mentally and emotionally. He is on a similar spiritual path. He gives me space to grow and evolve and I give him space to grow and evolve. He loves and adores me and I love and adore him. He accepts and loves my family as I accept and love his family. He is loved and respected by all as I am. We have a healthy sex life. He has a great sense of humor. We enjoy doing things together like traveling, shopping, going out for dinner and just talking. We live happily together to the good of all parties concerned. Thank you, thank you, thank you."

I fully accept

Signed   **Anne Marie Evers**

Dated   November, 2004

The process of doing Affirmations works within the Law of Attraction. This law, like all other natural laws is no respecter of person and works for everyone alike, similar to The Law of Gravity — when you drop something it falls, (unless you are in space). This law does not say, "Opps you have been a bad person, I will not work for you." It works every time for every person.

When you affirm, "I deserve and now have a loving, lasting, relationship which turns into marriage with the perfect person for me; I now attract my special life partner," and more, these are all positive Affirmations enforcing and magnifying these statements to attract more of the same to you. It is so important to do some thought watching and find out exactly where your thoughts are residing. We have between 50,000-60,000 thoughts that run through our minds daily. Do you ever wonder how many of those thoughts are:

(a) same as yesterday?

(b) negative?

(c) positive?

Do some *thought watching* and if you are not pleased where your thoughts are residing, you created them and you, and you alone, have the power to *uncreate* them.

The process of doing Affirmations is a twice daily procedure to receive your desires as affirmed. Take out your Master Affirmation and read it over every morning and evening, bringing in your 5 physical senses. Do this procedure until it manifests (that special life partner appears in your reality).

Affirmation Success!

I am living proof that Affirmations really work! I do them for every part of my life and one of the most important ones was that I attracted my third husband. I started doing my Master Affirmation as set out above in late 2004. I became a little discouraged when the end of 2005 came and went and I still had not met him. I thought to myself how can I teach this information to others if it is not working for me? Then I remembered what I teach—repetition, repetition, and repletion. So I kept on repeating my Master Affirmation daily and then early in 2006 I met Reggie my third husband. Oh yes, I have to admit I really had to work at it to keep my faith and belief that this was really happening.

You see the reason it took so long was when I started my Master Affirmation, Reggie was already married. Then sadly his wife passed away and later we met. I had ordered up (affirmed) for a husband and also someone to help me in my work especially in shipping and handling my products and he is even more than I ever imagined! We were married on June 8th, 2008 in my back yard and I have never been happier! (As I always say, "If it can work for me, it can work for anyone—you, you, and all of you!"

5. ANGEL CHAPEL

One day, a couple of years ago while having breakfast at Ricky's Restaurant, I said to my husband Reg, "What do you think about having a small Chapel in our backyard?" He said, "I think that would be great and I could even build it. I did build one house years ago you know."

Right then and there I grabbed a napkin and wrote an Affirmation on it saying that we deserved and now had a beautiful Angel Chapel in our backyard. I then asked Reg to read it over, and see if he agreed with it and if he did to sign which he did. Then I also signed and dated it.

Then we 'blew breath' into that Affirmation by taking action. We went to a lumber yard and asked one of the employees if they had any small play houses or small sheds. She showed us what they had and then suggested that we try another store. When Reg heard the name of the store, he exclaimed, "Oh one of my buddies just accepted the position of Manager there."

Off we went to that store and Reg's friend gave us a great deal on a kit for a playhouse. Then Reg put it together stick by stick, board by board and I even pounded a few nails. When he was finished he decided to make the grounds beautiful as well with a path leading up to The Angel Chapel.

Talk about Affirmations working ---I affirmed that we find the perfect size cross to put on the Chapel. The first Thrift Store we went to had about 50 wooden crosses, large enough to adorn this little Chapel. Reg finished the Chapel and grounds and to date we have had hundreds of people physically visit the Angel Chapel.

Reg says it is so exciting to see these folks coming in feeling sad and depressed and leaving The Angel Chapel with hope in their hearts and a spring in their step. He is thrilled to be a part of it. Many thousands of people have visited us on on-line @ www.annemariesangelchapel.com

So when people ask me, "Do Affirmation Really Work?" it brings tears to my eyes as I recall the wondrous results that I have received from doing my Affirmations Process, which is built on the 5 Building Blocks.

Do you want the Affirmation Process to work for you? It takes work and effort on your part. Remember the saying, "Effort In, Effort Out?"

Now when people ask Reggie, "Do Affirmations really work? Just ask Reggie! He says, "You bet they do!" He is now a firm believer!

6. HEALTH AFFIRMATION FOR PERFECT EYESIGHT

I was doing a Master Affirmation for perfect eyesight 20/20 vision for several months. Then I went for an Eye Exam and when the doctor said, "I am happy to tell you that you have cataracts in both eyes." I gasped and almost fell over. I said, "That is not what I hoped to hear, I hoped to hear that all I needed was glasses for driving." He replied, "Cataract Surgery has come a long way and these cataracts can be removed." His nurse immediately arranged for a surgeon to perform the surgery. I can tell you I was so scared, and FEAR welled up in my whole body.

So I started doing an Affirmation to disperse the fear. I used one of my Affirmation Tools from my Affirmation Toolbox Book and affirmed that I was free of this fear and that peace took over. I have to admit it worked, but still there were times that the fear would try and take over, and I would then use another tool from my Affirmation Tool box, the 'Cancel, Cancel Affirmation Tool Technique,' and completing it with the statement, "Successful surgery; healed eye; I am peaceful; I am safe; I see clearly."

When I spoke to my friend Peter Williams he said, "Well Dr. Anne Marie did you ever think of all the people you will meet along your journey and how you will have the opportunity to share your knowledge of Affirmations and help others?"

The doctor performed the surgery on my right eye and every morning and night I wrote out 77 times (another tool from my toolbox--the Saturation Affirmation Tool Process). "My right eye heals quickly and easily, perfect eyesight, 20/20 vision." I wrote these words out more than 77 times morning and evening and I brought in the FEELING that this was actually taking place in my body, for which I said, "Thank you, thank you, thank you." Then when I went back to the doctor 3 weeks later, he looked at my right eye and said, "Great! It is doing wonderful." I said, "You know doctor I am experiencing a bit of difficulty with my balance because one eye is so clear and the other is so cloudy. How long before you can fix the left eye?" He said, "Well actually I have a cancellation so I can do surgery on the left eye next week." Usually there is a wait period of several months between surgeries.

So I had the second surgery and all through it I was writing out my Saturation Affirmations 77 times in the morning and 77 times in the evening. When I checked back with the doctor both my eyes healed quickly and he was very pleased with the great results. When I was checked by the original doctor, he said. "Well, congratulations you now have better eyesight than most of us."

So my friend Peter was right, this journey took me through many places, some of fear, worry, happiness, relief and sharing my knowledge about the power of positive Affirmations. I shared the process of Affirmations with the nurses, receptionists, hospital nurses and doctors. I also donated copies of my Affirmation books to both offices, the hospital and I personally counseled 2 nurses about the power of properly done Affirmations. I certainly do believe in Affirmations and I believe in what I say on my radio shows, Affirmations When Properly Done Always Work *(sometimes not in our time frame or as we think they should)*. Of course the way I thought they would work was that I would be instantly and miraculously healed. What happened was that my Affirmation *did* manifest as affirmed by using the medical services of our highly skilled and trained doctors. I always use the Affirmation

Process as an *addition to* what your medical doctor and/or health practitioner and their treatment.

Check with your Doctor before you stop taking your Medications

One lady told me she felt so wonderful after doing Affirmations that she was going to stop taking her medication. I advised her strongly to go to her doctor and find out if the prescription for depression could be modified, but to keep on following her doctor's orders and do Affirmations as well.

Affirmations When Properly Done Always Work!

TESTIMONIALS FROM SOME READERS

Hello Dr. Evers

.... I am saying 'Thank you' on Behalf of all the People you Have Helped Worldwide that You do Not Know Even Exist through your Affirmation Books, radio shows and articles!!! And Now this incredible BOOK--Affirmation Toolbox!

I just wanted to say thank you, thank you, thank you for everything you do for the world! ! ! ! ! ! I am still so excited that I spoke to you!! You are my hero, my inspiration!! And putting together this new and exciting Affirmation Toolbox where we can go to the Table of Contents and select the exact Affirmation Tool that we need at that time and place is fabulous! It is so quick and easy — no searching for answers-they are all there and much more! I refer to your recent book as my Daily Recipe Book and always keep it handy. You are a great teacher! ! and please KNOW and REMEMBER THIS . . . Just because some of your followers don't let you know the great help of your Affirmations, books and writings and the miracles that happen . . . . it does not mean that your work is not worth Millions! Your work is so wonderful and is helping millions of people worldwide . . . people that you do not even know exist . . . . So--In the name of all these people, I tell you a great big THANK YOU! *God Bless. Much Love & gratitude. Maria C New York USA*

MANIFESTED THE CAR OF HER CHOICE USING ONE OF THE AFFIRMATION TOOLS

.... This is the Master Affirmation that I used to manifest my wonderful car! Please share with others that when you do your Master Affirmation specifically and properly they manifest as affirmed!

Master Affirmation for My Car

"I, Judith B deserve and now have purchased a 1993 Ford Escort GT in excellent condition, at the perfect price and fully loaded. It safe strong, reliable, attractive and economical. It has A/C and many other options. I own and use it to the good of all concerned. Thank you, thank you, thank you!"

I fully accept

Signed _____

Dated _____

Affirmations in General – Some More Testimonials

What some readers say--

.... I purchased one of your many wonderful Affirmation books approximately seven years ago. Over those years I have been affirming and receiving things constantly. From affirming a parking spot, to affirming large amounts of money, to affirming happiness and health to the people that are important to me in my life, a better job, happiness in my marriage, good health to my children — they now have all manifested for me. I believe the only reason Affirmations do not work for people is that they tend to give up on them. Persistence always pays off.

As you have always said, Anne Marie, Affirmations when properly done always work. I feel that one of the most important things people can do for themselves is learn how to forgive everyone and everything that has ever hurt them. From there, if you sincerely do this you can open doors to miracles. I know that I have. Thank you for everything you have done for me, my family, and everyone else you have blessed. Love, *Leslee, Movie business, North Vancouver, Canada*

. . . . Since discovering your book, my whole world has changed. I am a walking Affirmation. My entire outlook of my future has changed for the positive. I feel so great! Anne Marie, you do make a difference in this life. You have made a huge difference in mine. Your book is on my desk, your teachings are in my mind and heart, and you are in my thoughts and prayers. *V.K. Overseas*

. . . . I am a reader of one of your Affirmations books. I believe this is the most useful book I have ever purchased for myself. Many of the money attracting methods you teach in the book work perfectly for me. Thank you for making it available over the internet. Patty, South Africa

CUP EMPYTING FORGIVENESS AFFIRMATION TOOL

. . . . Hi beautiful Anne Marie. I just wanted to let you know how the Cup Emptying Course you teach in your Affirmation book is going. I have been doing the Cup Emptying Method (filling it with water) and visualizing all of my negative thoughts pouring into the cup from my eyes, ears and mouth. When that is complete for that day I take the cup to the sink and dump the water down the drain. When I first started doing it, the imaginary water came pouring out with great force. Now it seems to have just come out in small drips (that's amazing isn't it?)I am really enjoying this Exercise and will keep you posted as to the results. My health has improved and every day I feel better and better. I look forward to do this Affirmation Tool Exercise every day. I haven't even peeked ahead because I like the surprise of every day. *Much love Laverne*

AFFIRMATIONS EVEN HELP TO ATTRACT A SAILBOAT
Dear Dr. Anne

. . . . I love sailing and did not want to depend on friends to do it. I really wanted to have my own boat and sail whenever I wanted to. I used one of your Affirmation Tools for a sailboat about four months ago the way it says in the book, Affirmation Toolbox. Every morning I did my Affirmations faithfully. Then my partner decided that he too, wanted to sail and suggested we put our resources together and purchase one. Since I could not do it alone this was the perfect solution. We now own a brand new 26' Sailboat and are realizing our dream of sailing every weekend and we are doing it together! *"Jeanne M.*

'BIG MONEY TO ME NOW' METHOD BRINGS MONEY FROM UNUSUAL AND UNEXPECTED SOURCES---Help from Affirmations Toolbox

.... Since reading your Affirmation books, Affirmations and in particular your latest one Affirmation Toolbox they have become a very important part of my life. They have brought many positive changes to me, and I've been doing 'Big Money to Me Now' Method that you teach faithfully for the last few months. Money has started to come to me from unusual and unexpected sources. Also since doing the Affirmations, I have been able to let go of past, negative issues and new doors have opened. (I ordered up my soul mate!. . . .) and he arrived just as I ordered! So thank you, thank you, thank you. .. and many Blessings to you and your readers. *S. Singh, North Vancouver, BC*

Most Comprehensive, complete Book I have ever read on the Subject of Affirmations

.... I just **LOVE** your book on Affirmations. Affirmations Your Passport to Happiness is the most comprehensive and complete book I have ever read on the subject of Affirmations. You have completed a vast task and I believe it should be part of every child's education (and in the libraries for adults as well). As I grow and mature, I am aware more and more of the power of that unconscious field that creates all that we experience as our life. We do not comprehend and realize the power of thought and it is through the disciplines that you teach, Dr. Evers that thought can be focused and if the thoughts are benign, loving, forgiving and wish good for all including oneself, it will bring only joy, love and success in the outward experience. Also congratulations are in order for your latest book, Affirmation Toolbox with over a hundred simple, yet very powerful Affirmation Tools. *Jon George, New Westminster, BC Canada*

You Really Have Touched on a Prosperity Formula with your Affirmation Toolbox Book!

.... Thank you so much Anne Marie. In the last 3 weeks since I have been doing the Money Affirmations that you teach in your books and my practice has doubled!

You really have touched on a Prosperity Formula here! Once Dan and I get ourselves cozily settled in our new home we would like to have you visit and do some seminars. Much caring, *Tammi-Lynn, Toronto, Canada*

Affirmations Find a Buyer for Motor Home

.... This is a Testimonial Dr. Evers. Following your instructions in your Affirmation Toolbox Book, I must report the outcome. Once again Affirmations have worked for me. For two days I used your Affirmation Tools and I affirmed to find a buyer for our motor home. I placed an add on Craigslist and yesterday when we came back from camping someone had emailed me expressing a desire to view the motor home. He liked it so much that he bought it on the spot! Simply Amazing! *Richard Denault, Maple Ridge, Canada*

Affirmations A Magical Book to Creating a Wonderful Life--Excellent Positive Reading

.... This book called Affirmation Toolbox is a great tool for positive thinking and learning. Any person that would like to learn new techniques regarding how to go from negative to positive thinking should read this book. It is written in a clear manner and provides step-by-step exercises for the reader to use. Excellent book and an excellent author. D.B. 2011

.... W O W! All I can say is 'WOW!' Those Affirmations really do work! My doctor is very pleased with my success in getting rid of unwanted pounds. I created my own positive CD using my own voice as you suggested. I listen to it both going to work and coming home from work. It certainly is a very powerful Affirmation Tool. Thank you for writing the Affirmation Toolbox. I find it very helpful and refer to it almost daily. Very impressive! Cheers Richard, Computer Technician, Washington, DC USA

CLEAR, SEARCH & RETRIEVE AFFIRMATION TOOL

.... I passed my Real Estate Exam with flying colors using some of the different Affirmation Tools that you teach in your Affirmation Toolbox book. I did an Affirmation as follows: "I, Donald deserve and now have passed my Real Estate Exam with good marks. I am happy to the good of all parties concerned. Thank you, thank you, thank you." Then I did as you teach and--signed and dated it. When I did that I had a feeling that I had really entered into a contract with my Creator! What a great feeling and oh yes, I knew beyond a shadow of a doubt that I passed that exam. Now I am sharing my new-found information with others who are interested to learn. *Daniel, Now Successful Real Estate Agent, Toronto, ON Canada*

AFFIRMATIONS HELP REBUILD OUR MARRIAGE

.... We are working on re-building our marriage and doing it with the help of your Affirmation Program, love and support. We are using the Relationship Affirmation Tools you teach in your Affirmation Toolbox book and already seeing fantastic and sometimes unbelievable success. With many thanks and loving thoughts. *Ben, Manager, Hamilton, ON*

.... Since reading your book and watching you on television, I thought to myself, "Why not give it a whirl? It certainly cannot hurt. I began affirming divine order, love and peace in my relationship and love life. What a HUGE difference. We are even discussing having another child. I can't thank you enough. I think it is important to keep on encouraging people in good, satisfying relationships and marriages to affirm continued love, peace and joy. I am glad you see it that way too! *Colleen, Winnipeg, Manitoba*

Dear Dr. Anne Marie   Peggy Passed her Exam!

. . . . Thank you so much, words are never enough! When I contacted you I was very nervous and some-what discouraged as my instructor told me there was a high percentage of people that did not pass this particu-lar Exam. After speaking with you, I decided to put my hopes on the information you shared with me and on myself that I could muster up the courage to write the exam and pass with good marks. I followed your sugges-tions exactly as you taught me in our counseling sessions, Affirmation Tools and books. I used the Affirmation Tool - CLEAR, SEARCH & RETRIEVE that you taught me. First of all I completely and totally relaxed taking several deep breaths, breathing OUT my fear and worry and breath-ing IN peace, joy and knowingness.

When I felt that part was complete, I started with the first question and the first part of the process. I said to myself, "Clear," and then I visualized completely clearing my mind of all worry and chatter. Then I said, "Search." After that I visualized my mind going into the filing cabinet of my mind and locating the file that said, 'Answers to the Pre-Test for Peggy, June 1st, 2011." When I felt my mind had located the correct file with all the answers, I said 'Retrieve.' Then I visualized the correct answers being transported from the files of my mind into my present memory and being there for me to locate and use. I did this with every question. Somehow because I had this Affirmation Tool and knew you were also affirming with me, I was not the least bit nervous. I took the Test with 100 questions and I only missed 5 questions. I passed with the high marks I had affirmed. Again I cannot Thank you enough. I am now a true believer. Such is the power of focused, concentrated thoughts, Affirmations, Visualizations and Affirmation Tools! *Peggy Student of the Universe.*

The Fear Zoo Exercise Worked for Tiffany

. . . . My daughter Tiffany who is a 3rd grader had a wonderful experience with doing Affirmations. She followed your instructions from your Affirmation Toolbox Book and did the Fear Zoo Exercise. She visualized her fear of heights as a large giraffe named Gerry and put it into a beautiful cage in a Fear Zoo. She did this by drawing a picture of the giraffe, brightly colored it and then pasted it on construction paper. She took straws and pasted them over the drawing which made the bars of a cage. She made the cage very pretty with flowers, leaves and greenery. She would go (in her mind) and talk to it every day. The more she talked about her fear to Gerry, the more he listened, asked questions and answered her questions and the fear lessened and actually faded away. Last month the whole family went on a vacation and I am so happy to report she participated in every event, even the ones that included going to exhibits, etc. which necessitated traveling on elevators, going up stairs and heights, etc. This is such a gift to our whole family as well as Tiffany as we always dreaded that part of our trip and now we ALL look forward to our entire trip with happy anticipation We cannot thank you enough, Yes we all believe in Affirmations and we are doing them as a family regularly for other things, like family vacations, outings, etc. *Josie and Family*

Dear Anne Marie -- Affirmations Go to School in Lunch Boxes

. . . . Thank you for sending me your Children's Affirmation of the Day. It reminds me to send my children to school with a short note from me in their lunch boxes, reminding them how much I love them, what is happening that day after school and what I appreciate about them. I have also included one of your daily Affirmations. When I skip a day or so they really notice and ask me to start sending them again. Thanks for the daily reminder of how important affirmations are to our children and ourselves. With gratitude. *Kelly, Appreciative mom in Vancouver, WA*

AFFIRMATIONS HELPED ME OVERCOME MY FEAR OF FLYING

. . . . When I met you, Anne Marie Evers several years ago, I was terrified of flying and I needed to go on a trip with my husband. When we talked about my fear you suggested that I do an Affirmation. You helped me write out an Affirmation for helping me overcome my fear of flying. I used it and it worked. I kept it in my wallet. I also found out information about airplanes, safety measures and flying. Since that time I have flown on many flights and always carry in my wallet that Affirmation that you wrote for me that day years ago. It has accompanied me on all my flights. I have to share a story with you about one of my latest trips on a plane. It was a very small plane with about 20 or so passengers. When flying we hit an air pocket where we all of a sudden dropped what seemed like hundreds of feet. Everyone started screaming and the flight attendant who was serving hot coffee landed on the floor in the aisle at the front of the plane.

Several of us passengers got up and grabbed the serving cart to keep it from flying around and/or hitting her. The flight attendant looked up and what really got me was the terror I saw in her eyes as she started to pick herself up. It was almost as if she was frozen watching and waiting for the serving cart to hit her. Also the screaming and fear of the other passengers was what got to me, not the actual flying. When getting off that little airplane the pilot said to me, "I guess you will never fly again?" I said, "Oh it wasn't too bad. We all survived! Now if I can survive and live to tell the story that is going a long way on my Flying journey. Do Affirmations and positive thinking work? I am here to say they do! Thank you Anne Marie for sharing this very important information that helped me immensely. And thank you for writing your latest Affirmation Toolbox book, which I am presently reading and using the Affirmation Tools with great success! *Nicki, Reformed Terrified Flyer, Vancouver, BC*

Affirmations When Properly Done Always Work!

AUTHOR'S COMMENTS

Please drop me a line with your comments. I always LOVE to hear from you. It is my hope and prayer that some of the information offered herein will encourage, uplift and give you HOPE. I trust that you have enjoyed your journey of uncovering and discovering simple, yet powerful Affirmation Tools to help you on your journey of life. I look forward to hearing from you very soon. And remember:

Affirmations When Properly Done Always Work!

I sincerely support you in realizing your heart's fondest desires.

Love, Happiness and Many Blessings,

Dr. Anne Marie Evers

www.annemarieevers.com
www.affirmationtoolbox.com
www.cardsoflife.com
www.kidspower.ca

BOOKS
by Dr. Anne Marie Evers

Affirmations: Your Passport to Happiness & Much More -8th *edition*
Affirmations: Your Passport to Lasting, Loving Relationships

Affirmations: Your Passport to Prosperity/Money
Affirmation Beauty Book.
The above books are *also* available in e-book form:

Wake up . . . . Live the Life You Love In Spirit – Co-author with Dr. Deepak Chopra & Dr. Wayne Dyer

OTHER PRODUCTS AND SERVICES

Affirmation Coaching by Dr. Anne Marie

The Cards of Life
The Cards of Life Certification Course
Kids Affirmation Program (KAP) Grades 1-3
Kids Affirmation Program (KAP) Grades 4-6
Affirmations 101 – A Primer

Dr. Deepak Chopra and Dr. Evers
Kids Affirmation Club
James Harvey's CD
Numerous other e-books

18436027R00164

Made in the USA
San Bernardino, CA
14 January 2015